THE LINK
WITNEY LIBRARY

HOW TO WRITE
STORIES, POEMS, REPORTS,
LETTERS AND EMAILS

ANNE FAUNDEZ
WES MAGEE
CELIA WARREN

QED Publishing

Copyright © QED Publishing 2009

First published in the UK in 2009 by
QED Publishing
A Quarto Group company
226 City Road
London EC1V 2TT
www.qed-publishing.co.uk

All rights reserved. No part of this publication may be reproduced, stored
in a retrieval system, or transmitted in any form or by any means, electronic,
mechanical, photocopying, recording, or otherwise, without the prior permission
of the publisher, nor be otherwise circulated in any form of binding or cover
other than that in which it is published and without a similar condition being
imposed on the subsequent purchaser.

A Catalogue record for this book is available from the British Library.

ISBN 978 1 84835 334 3

Authors Anne Faundez, Wes Magee, Celia Warren
Designer Jackie Palmer
Editor Louisa Somerville
Illustrator Tim Loughead

Publisher Steve Evans
Creative Director Zeta Davies

Printed and bound in China

Website information is correct at time of going to press.
However, the publishers cannot accept liability for any
information or links found on third-party websites.

Words in **bold**
are explained in the
glossary on page 116.

CONTENTS

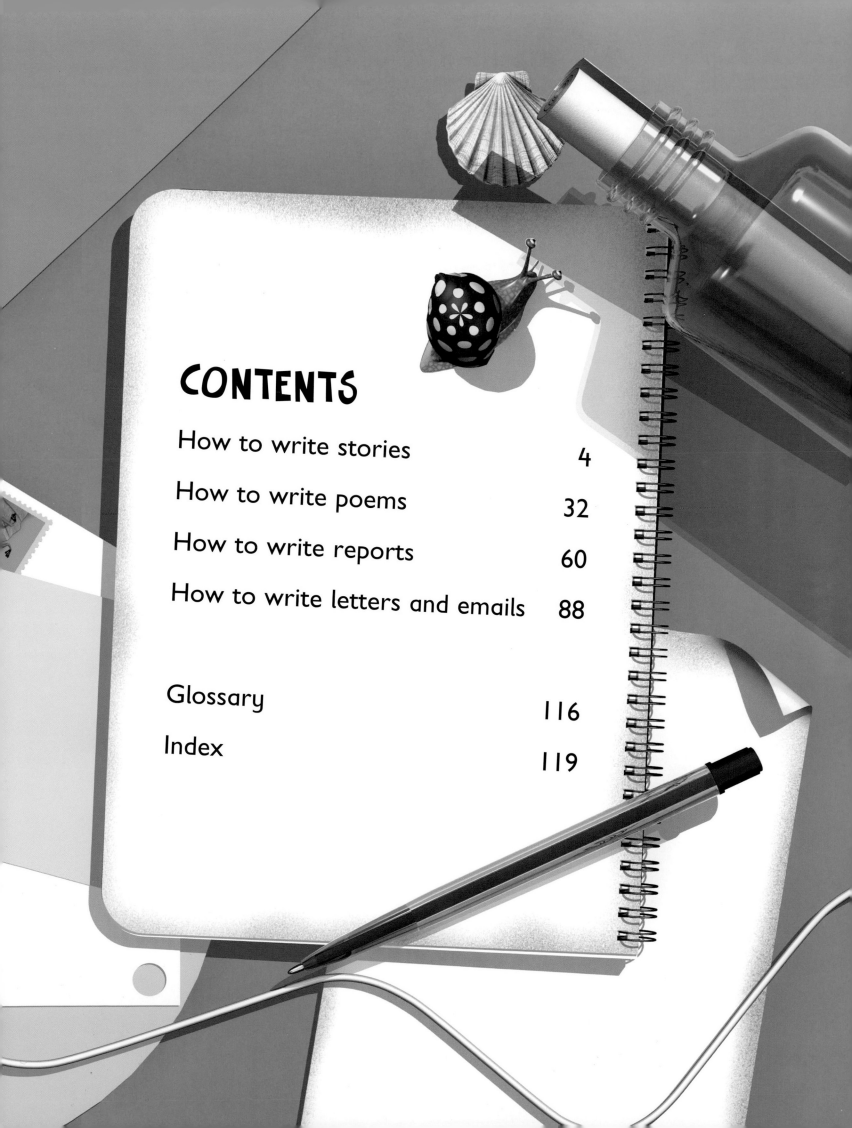

Tips and techniques from a real writer

How To Write
STORIES

Pin your ideas to the page!

Now YOU can write:

- believable characters
- brilliant plots
- gripping cliff-hangers

CONTENTS

STORY GENRES

Anyone who makes up stories and writes them down is an **author**. You can be an author, too! The wonderful thing about being an author is that you can be anyone, go anywhere, do anything you like. If you want to sprout wings and fly or be a deep-sea diver, you can! You can do anything in your imagination. If you turn it into a story, then others can share your adventures in **fiction**. Take a look at some of the **genres** of story – but don't forget, some books can fit into more than one genre.

Did you know?
The name Wendy did not exist until the author J.M. Barrie wrote Peter Pan just over 100 years ago. He invented the name after he heard a young child say "my wendy", meaning "my friendy" (my friend).

- **Fairy stories, legends and folk tales**
  Well-known traditional tales – including *Goldilocks and the Three Bears* and *The Frog Prince* – and **legends** such as those featuring *Robin Hood* and *Odysseus*.

- **Fables and parables**
  Stories with a moral or a message, including such Bible stories as *The Prodigal Son* and *The Good Shepherd*, and Aesop's **fables**, such as *The Hare and the Tortoise*.

- **Historical**
  Stories set in the past, such as *Goodnight Mr Tom* **by Michelle Magorian.** They can be about real or fictional events.

Some authors' fictional **characters** are so convincing that they become as much a part of life as if they were real people. You'd know Winnie the Pooh, Alice in Wonderland or Harry Potter if you met them in the street, wouldn't you?

- **Sci-fi (short for science fiction)**
  Stories inspired by scientific developments. They are usually set in the future and often involve aliens. The *Artemis Fowl* books by Eoin Colfer are sci-fi stories.

- **Fantasy**
  Stories whose characters or events are not based in reality. The reader must accept the writer's **fantasy** world. *The Lion, the Witch and the Wardrobe* by C.S. Lewis is a fantasy story.

- **Adventure and mystery**
  Stories about exciting and mystifying events, where readers try to solve the mystery along with the characters. *The Scarecrow and his Servant* by Philip Pullman is an adventure story.

Tips

- It's often best to write the sort of story that you would enjoy reading yourself.
- Read as many books in different genres as you can. The more you read, the more your own writing will improve.

- **Graphic stories**
  Stories, such as those about the adventures of Tintin or Asterix, told in pictures with words in speech bubbles and captions.

GATHERING IDEAS

Ideas for stories are everywhere. Something you see, hear or dream may spark off the inspiration for a story or, at least, an incident or a character. It's not always convenient to sit down and write straight away, so make notes when ideas occur to you.

Ideas notebook

Keep a notebook beside your bed or in your pocket – with a pen, of course. Jot down anything that pops into your head, even just a word. It could come in handy when creating a character or situation for a new story. You could write down:

- an overheard snippet of conversation (but don't eavesdrop!)
- bits of dreams – as soon as you wake up.
- something funny, unusual or interesting you see while walking in the park, such as a parent training a dog to find her children, a kite getting stuck in a tree or a child's ice cream toppling on to a toddler's head.
- a series of words that pop into your head from nowhere. For example:

"Floppy poppy! Well, blow me down!"

Tip

When you're next in the mood for writing, open your notebook and see what you scribbled down – the seeds of ideas for stories. Now you can 'water' the seeds and watch them grow!

In the news

Newspapers are a great source of story ideas. Most news stories involve people (who can become your story's characters). For example, a new planet is discovered. Who are the scientists involved? What are they like? If the newspaper doesn't tell you, invent their characters for yourself.

Copycat?

Rewriting a newspaper story does not make it your own. The writer has the **copyright** of their article. You don't have the right to copy what they have written but you can take a real-life piece of news and draw information from it for a different story. So you could turn the discovery of a dinosaur into a story about an archaeologist who digs up a dinosaur skeleton that comes to life after everyone at the museum has gone home. This turns **facts** into fiction.

Springboard

Take a few words from a newspaper story or headline and use them as a story title. You are only using the words for the title, so your story will be nothing like the one in the newspaper. Here are some made-up headlines to start you off:

• Prince pays the price
• Polly the parrot keeps mum
• Cheesy does it!
• Smallest mammal discovered
• Rover to the rescue!

Tip

All stories involve a character – either human or animal – who has a problem that must be solved. Before you start writing, ask yourself: who is my story's main character and what is his or her problem?

Tip

Change the characters' names from those in real life – to something memorable, if possible. Professor Trudie Spligwort is quite a catchy name!

the daily news

NEW PLANET DISCOVERED

FROM FACT TO FICTION

It can be hard to get started with story writing. People often say, "Write about what you know". Writing from your own experience gives you confidence, but you can also describe what happens to others. Because your brain gathers knowledge from the world around you all the time, you don't need to have broken a bone yourself to have a character break a leg!

'I know...' plus 'what if...?'

Here's a way to write a story that moves from what you know to what you can only imagine. Using a pencil, write an account of something that has happened in your life, as if you were telling a friend or writing a diary. Read it through, with a pen handy. Ask yourself "What if ...?" and use the pen to change some things slightly and others dramatically, turning facts into fiction. Maybe you could introduce a fantasy element. Here's an example:

Edit the **text** so that the **narrative** flows more smoothly.

This morning, when I opened the curtains the sky was green. My mouth fell open. ~~it was pouring with rain. I was annoyed as~~ had planned a M ~~my~~ friend Danny and I ~~were planning a~~ picnic by the river. Instead we ~~decided to go to the cinema.~~ but the voice that answered I rang Danny ~~and we arranged to meet at the bus-~~ sounded nothing like him. ~~stop and get the twelve-thirty bus into town.~~

Tip

In your writing, it is better to show than to tell. For example, 'I was annoyed' tells the reader how the author felt, but 'My mouth fell open' is much more expressive. It shows that the author was astounded without actually saying it.

Check that your new words make sense alongside the original words that you're keeping.

Copy the start of your new story onto a fresh sheet of paper, like this:

Springboard

Write a story that begins and ends with the same phrase, such as:
- I never did like carrots.
- It was the first and last day I ever met my cousin.
- Dogs understand more than we think.

This morning, when I opened the curtains, the sky was green. My mouth fell open. My friend Danny and I had planned a picnic by the river. I rang Danny but the voice that answered sounded nothing like him.

The story now has lots of possibilities. Danny sounds different.

- Will he look different, too?
- Has Danny turned into someone else?
- Is the sky really green and, if so, why? Or are the writer's senses confused?

Ask yourself some 'what', 'where', 'why' and 'who' questions about your own story. Jot down ideas, so that you know roughly where the story is going and how it will end. Then write the rest of the story before your enthusiasm dwindles.

Springboard

- Imagine yourself shrinking or growing so that a familiar environment becomes threatening or dangerous.

- Have a fantasy character living your life. For example: what happens when a snowman eats porridge or sits next to the radiator at school?

BUILDING A STORY

Writing a story is a bit like building a house. You gather your materials – your words – but before you begin building you need a design. Here are the things you need for your story design:

Protagonist:
Drizzle the wizard
        or Wikedelia
           the witch?
Other characters:
Crumble the Cat,
Freaky Frog,
Elfrida
always mumbling under her breath, allergic to feathers?

Setting

The setting is the time and place. It could be another planet in the future, a school or a pharaoh's palace. You may find it helps to imagine the setting as a theatre. Picture a stage for your character-actors with several backdrops for different scenes.

TIME: 3000 BCE
PLACE: Egypt
SCENES: The throne room of the Pharaoh's palace; a holy temple; the dark, winding corridors of a pyramid; a barge on the Nile.

Theme

The theme is the story's message. It may be something that the reader thinks about after they have read the story. For example, the theme may be 'you can overcome fear' or 'bad people don't win'.

Characters

The main character is called the **protagonist**. Try to make your readers care about this person and identify with them, which means being able to understand and share the character's thoughts and feelings. You can create characters that oppose the protagonist, or who influence events. (Use contrasting names to avoid your readers getting confused.) Use **dialogue** to show their personalities. Picture them: how do they speak? what habits do they have?

Don't create too many characters for you to remember!

Plot

What happens in which order and why, and with what outcome is called a **plot**. Making a timeline helps you to work out the plot. Mark the story's main events along the timeline.

Kit goes on holiday | Feels bored and lonely | Meets magic horse | Kit and horse dive into sea | They reach island | Kit meets pirates | Finds treasure

From start... to finish

Once you have your story's setting, characters and plot, it's time to start 'building'! Your story will have three parts: a beginning, a middle and an end.

Beginning

Make the start of your story short. Involve the reader straight away without too much description or detail. A good attention-grabber is to start with **direct speech**.

"Hey – that's *my* bike you're riding," shouted Jack.
The girl wobbled for a second as she glanced over her shoulder.
"Well, it's mine now," she said.

We learn several things:
The main character is called Jack.
There's a confrontation and problem to overcome.
Jack doesn't know the girl. (The author hasn't used her name – yet!)

Middle

Next, the characters develop and things happen in a string of connected events. The characters' actions influence events, which may, in turn, change the characters' feelings, attitudes or even their whole lives!

End

It is important to tie up all 'loose ends'. Don't leave your reader thinking, "But what about such-and-such?" Provide a satisfying outcome. It must leave the protagonist (and readers who care about him or her) feeling better off than at the start and with most – if not all – problems solved. We should be able to close the book content that we know what happened to all the characters.

Tip

A page of text could cover anything from a minute to half a lifetime, depending on the story length. Make the plot unfold fast enough to keep your readers' attention but slow enough for them to get to know the characters and share the action.

Springboard

Try building a story from these materials:

THEME: Lost SETTING: Fairground
PROTAGONIST: Young boy or girl
PLOT: Boy/girl has run away because they're unhappy. By the end of the story, the child is back home and the reader knows why the child was unhappy, how he or she was found and why the child is happier than he or she was before.

CREATING CHARACTERS

Creating a character is like making a new friend!

Believable characters are vital to a good story. They should seem like real people, so remember that nobody is all good or all bad. Even the nastiest character might be kind to dogs or love their mum! Even the nicest character has a weak spot — a streak of jealousy maybe. You decide — but beware! As your characters become more real, it can be hard to make them stay in the plot.

Character file

Keep a fact-file about each key character. The more you include, the more you will get to know them. Include their colouring, age, height and build, hobbies, pets, favourite food, sports team or anything else of interest. You could also note their greatest disappointment or ambition. Once their personalities are established, the characters will seem real in your story.

GRANDPA GREGOR'S CHARACTER FILE:

70 years old and frail; very straight, white hair; rimless specs; usually bent over but straightens up when speaking; listens to brass band music on his MP3 player; would like to have played the trombone.

Tip

Some friends may take offence at appearing in your stories, so if you base a character on someone you know, make sure to disguise them. If it's a boy, make him a girl, and so on. Change other details, such as their age, hair colour or height.

Showing emotion

People's facial expressions and body language reveal what they are feeling. Imagine your character. Then show rather than tell your reader about the character's feelings through their actions, reactions, dialogue and body language.

TELL: Raj was unhappy.
SHOW: Raj strolled slowly, his head down and shoulders hunched. He frowned hard and bit his lip.

Note: When showing, the adjective 'unhappy' doesn't appear. Nor does the verb 'cry' but we know Raj was close to tears!

ACTIVITY

Describe your own bedroom. Include details that inform the reader about you: your age, gender, interests, family and friends.

Environment

Sometimes we learn about a character from their environment:

'The bedroom was untidy but, nevertheless, had an orderliness about it. A pile of pony books on the floor beside the unmade bed were sorted by size. A caged hamster shared a bookshelf with a cuddly toy rabbit that had obviously been well squeezed for most of its owner's ten years. Shoved to the back of a small desk lay a half-written letter. The depth of dust it lay under suggested it was unlikely ever to see the inside of an envelope.'

ACTIVITY

Describe Raj doing different things in different moods. Choose an activity and an emotion from each list.

Activity:
Playing with friends
Eating dinner
Climbing a steep hill
Water-skiing
Walking around the shops

Emotion:
Excited
Bored
Impatient
Lonely
Afraid

What's in a name?

Authors often pick names that reflect a character's looks or personality, such as Mr Happy, Penny Sweet or Old Mrs Longtooth. Choose unusual names to make it easier for you – and your readers – to remember who's who. For example, Jeannie Blacklake is more memorable than Jane Black.

Tip

Use an online search-engine to find more ideas for names. Some authors choose names because of their meanings. For example 'Peter' means steadfast, strong and dependable. This website lists names and their meanings: www.behindthename.com

Springboard

Write a story that shows how a person changes because of what happens to them, such as overcoming a fear. Choose a name that suits the character and situation, such as Sally Fairweather or Daniel Strong.

MINDMAPPING

Each of the world's six billion people has at least one story to tell. If you add to that six billion imaginations, that makes limitless ideas! Here are some ways of coming up with plots and planning how they will develop:

Mindmapping

Take a single word, and write down absolutely anything relating to it. Give yourself just five minutes and *don't think too hard*!

Start with one of these words:
PAPER WALLS SPACE WATER

Choose one thought that you've come up with and do a further **mindmap** around that.

Now, think of an incident that involves one of your ideas. This incident can form part of a story or you can develop the whole plot around it.

Good planning

Creating problems and solving each in turn makes for a good plot. As you plan your plot you will see how, as in real life, there isn't always one 'right' thing to do. Your characters will reach crossroads and have to choose a direction. Add a Happy Ending – even if there are tears on the way – or your readers will never forgive you!

What's the plot?

Plots usually involve one or both of the following:

- Thwarted ambition: someone or something stops the hero from getting what they want. They want to get from A to B but there are obstacles in the way.
- An emotional issue: a problem that involves a person's feelings and affects their lives. The hero goes on a 'personal journey' throughout the story. (This might also involve an actual journey to another place, such as a new home.)

confetti

newspaper ← PAPER →

* paper hat could stop sunstroke ← origami → * paper dart to send a message

* paper cup collects water from a fountain, rain-cloud or cave roof to save someone from dying of thirst

Storyboarding

One helpful way to plan the plot is by **storyboarding**. Draw a series of boxes: one for each **paragraph**, if it's a short story; one for each **chapter** if it's a **novel**. In each box sketch the main event, as if it was an episode from a film. Use these pictures as a prompt for your writing. Or, write notes to remind you what will happen at each stage of the story. For example, here is a storyboard plan for *Little Red Riding Hood*:

Springboard

Make a storyboard for your favourite story or fairy tale. You don't need to use full *sentences*, just briefly jot down – or sketch – the main events in order.

Little Red Riding Hood

Mother tells Little Red Riding Hood to put on cloak and take cake to Grandma who is ill in bed on other side of forest.	LRRH in wood, stops to picks flowers on way, not noticing a wolf spying on her.	Wolf asks where she is going. She tells him where and why, and he bids farewell and disappears.
LRRH arrives at G'ma's and finds her looking odd: eyes too big, ears too big ; wolf fobs her off ("All the better to see / hear you with"). LRRH mentions G'ma's huge teeth.	G'ma says "All the better to eat you with" – leaps from bed to attack LRRH who sees wolf is dressed up in G'ma's nightie.	LRRH screams and her dad (who is a woodman felling trees nearby) arrives with axe and kills wolf. They find G'ma shut in wardrobe.

DECISIONS, DECISIONS

Before you start writing you must decide about viewpoint (whether you, yourself, are in the story – or not) and **tense** (whether you will be writing in the past or present tense).

Point of view

From whose viewpoint are you writing?

- You can be an observer, rather as if you were watching a film. If so, you will write in the 'third person': *he, she, they, his, her, their* are useful pronouns.

- You can write as one of the characters, as if you were inside the story. If so, you will be writing in the 'first person': *I, me, my; we, us, our* are useful pronouns.

Past or present?

Are you telling the story in the past or present tense?

- The past tense is the most usual and perhaps the easiest way of story telling: *He went…they chose…it was fun…*

- The present tense is less usual but can be useful – especially as a contrast, for a character relating an event or a dream: *I am…I choose…It is fun…*

ACTIVITY

Read the opening lines of some stories you have enjoyed. What have the authors said, and how have they said it? Which viewpoint have they taken? Did they write in the past or present tense? Plan an opening sentence, or paragraph, that will grab your readers by the throat. Rewrite it, changing the viewpoint and tense. How does it affect your writing's impact?

TIP

Even if you are writing fantasy, it must be believable to your readers. Make up the 'rules' for your fantasy world – and stick to them. If your character suddenly sprouts wings to escape from a lion, that's too easy a way out. On the other hand, the character could ride on the back of a winged creature to escape.

Symbols

Before you begin to write, you must also decide if you will use **symbols** in your story. Symbols are things that stand for something. Colours are often used as symbols. For example, the colour red may symbolize danger. In the story of *Little Red Riding Hood*, her red cloak warns the reader of trouble ahead. Symbols are not always colours. For example, a dove is a symbol of peace and love, like the dove in the Bible story of *Noah's Ark*.

Animal symbols

Animals often symbolize human character types – a lion is usually bold; a peacock, proud; and so on. You can use them in stories to reinforce the type of character they are. Or you can make them behave the opposite to their stereotype: like the nervous Lion in *The Wizard of Oz* or Kenneth Grahame's gentle, friendly Reluctant Dragon.

Weather symbols

Weather that echoes a character's feelings can be used to create atmosphere. If your hero is unhappy, rain might reflect that sadness, just as sunshine could reflect a character's happiness and joy. Fog could reinforce a character's feelings of being lost or confused.

Select one of the titles below, or make up your own. Then choose some symbols to plan the story around.

- Red Snow
- The Lion Who Was Afraid
- Bottled Sunshine

Springboard

The Cat and The Broomstick

Black Hat Stories

Rainy Day Spells

ACTIVITY

Use weather or animal symbols in a fantasy story, such as one about a talking animal or a superhero, or an underground world that nobody's discovered before. Try writing The Country Where the Sun Never Shone. Why doesn't it shine? Who arrives to change all that?

PACE AND TIMING

Stories are often about journeys: from place to place or through time. There are also emotional and personal journeys, as characters deal with events. **Pace** and timing are useful tools for inviting the reader to join the journey.

The journey starts

It's a good idea to work out roughly how many words your story will be before you start. Then you can decide how many words to use to set the scene and introduce the characters. If your story will be 1000 words long in total, the beginning will probably be no more than 200 words.

Setting the pace

Deciding how to divide up the text across the whole piece of writing is called pacing. It is no good writing lots of detail for the first three-quarters of your story and then having to hurry the story-telling at the end.

Speed up and slow down

Pace also refers to how you tell the story. Vary the pace of your story-telling to avoid sounding monotonous.

ACTIVITY

Write two different openings to a story with a maximum of 200 words each.

1. Introduce the main character, starting with their birth. Include something remarkable, such as being born in a strange place. By the end, the character is 12 years old and in the here-and-now.

2. The character is 12 years old already. It could be an ordinary day that becomes extraordinary, or a special day for them. Help the reader to find out as much as possible about the character in 200 words.

How do the things we learn about the character differ between the first and second version? Which is more detailed? Are there more of the character's thoughts and feelings in the second?

- Long sentences, with **subclauses** and commas, slow down the story-telling.
- Words with long vowel sounds — oa, ee, ai — also relax the pace.
- Short sentences or phrases speed up the pace and add excitement.

The long and short of it

Read these two paragraphs. Each contains just 42 words, but the first covers more than 60 years, the other, less than 60 seconds.

Over sixty years, I had crossed every continent. I allowed my gaze to wander the length and depth of the wide blue sky. Every vapour trail seemed to lead away from me, far away to the distant horizon, inviting me to follow.

Suddenly there was a bang on the roof. Crash! Right above my head. I gave a yelp. A flash of orange outside the window made me recoil. My throat tightened. I struggled to swallow. "It can't be!" I croaked. But it was.

Tip

When you describe things, try to involve all five senses: touch, sight, sound, taste and smell.

Time phrases

A way of showing a passage of time is to use a time **phrase**. 'Shortly' and 'soon' mean much the same, but varying the phrases you use will spice up your writing. Here are some useful time phrases:

- soon
- shortly
- it was some time before
- before long
- meanwhile
- within the hour
- two weeks later
- after a while
- the following afternoon
- the next day
- until then
- over the next few days
- at first
- at last
- suddenly
- all at once
- just at that moment
- long ago
- as fast as
- for a second
- while
- during
- no sooner had... than...

Springboard

Write a story based on one of these journeys:

- Through the tunnel
- Over the rainbow
- Below the surface

Include at least one unusual form of transport – anything from a camel train to a parachute.

21

BREAKING WRITER'S BLOCK

Have you ever woken up bursting with a desire to write and found your brain won't join in – you have no ideas of what to write about, your mind is a blank? All writers get this from time to time. It's known as writer's block. Here are some ideas to kick-start your story-writing…

Better late than never

A fool and his/her money are soon parted

Absence makes the heart grow fonder

Choose a **proverb** or saying and plan a story that proves its truth. Here are some to start you off…

Where there's a will there's a way

Never, never, never…

Parents and teachers tell us things that we MUST NOT do! Mindmap a never-never list, for example:

NEVER TELL ANYONE ABOUT THE TIGER

NEVER TOUCH THE RED BUTTON

NEVER GO THROUGH THE GREEN GATE

NEVER PICK UP A SPOTTED SNAIL

Choose one of the warnings and decide what happens when your main character ignores it!

Disaster!

In real life, stories often revolve around an accident or a mistake. Describe an accident that happened to you or that you caused. It can be as small as tripping over a shoelace or dropping a take-away meal, or as big as a car crash or falling off a swing. Add a little imagination and poetic licence (the author's 'right' to change things slightly). Can you develop it into a story?

Or try one of these titles*:

- A Broken Ankle
- Cat Catastrophe
- Mistaken Identity
- The Forgotten Letter
- Wrong Time; Wrong Place

* These are working titles – a title to call your story while you are writing it. It's often best to leave the final title until your story is complete. It should be one that intrigues people, making them want to read your story, but without giving too much away.

Tip

When developing an idea, try to think as widely as possible of ways of interpreting your seed of an idea so that it will grow beautifully. Use a spidergram to mindmap words and phrases.

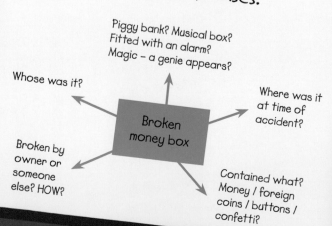

Piggy bank? Musical box? Fitted with an alarm? Magic – a genie appears?

Whose was it?

Where was it at time of accident?

Broken money box

Broken by owner or someone else? HOW?

Contained what? Money / foreign coins / buttons / confetti?

Springboard

Have a go at automatic writing. That is writing where you pick up your pen and write whatever comes into your head. You might even start by writing the same word over and over, until another pops into your head. The point is you ARE writing and – like an artist sketching before painting – a part of your automatic writing may grow into a story.

STORIES IN CHAPTERS

Short stories are fun to write – but how about a **novel** or **novella**? Here are some of the good things about writing a longer story.

You can...

- develop characters in greater depth, until they seem as real as your friends.
- take your characters through more experiences and to more locations.
- spend longer describing the setting and create different moods to complement the action.

One way to start...

If the idea of a novel is scary, try writing a series of short stories about one character, with a plot thread that links the stories. Join them as chapters in one book to create an **episodic** novel. Make sure that the plot is resolved in the final chapter.

For example, you might have a character who plays pranks on people. Each chapter – a story in its own right – tells of a trick he's played. At the same time, all those who have had tricks played on them, prepare to get their own back. They build up their friendship and plan revenge. The story reaches a climax as the joker is tricked in return.

ACTIVITY

Create a character with a problem – such as a girl who is struggling with homework. In trying to solve her problem, she creates a second one and so on. For example, her friend comes round and spills orange juice on both their books. In Chapter 3 they wipe their books, not knowing that the cloth has been used for bleach and they bleach the sofa... and so they go on until, in the final chapter, the problems are solved.

Tip

If you use a word-processing program to write on a computer it makes it easy to cut and paste text. It means you can add a chapter in the middle of the book, if you want, without any rewriting.

Chapter know-how

As you add more detail to any story, it will get longer and you can divide it into chapters. Make sure each chapter ends on a cliffhanger – a tantalizing line that makes the reader want to turn the page and read on. The start of each chapter must grab their attention, too, just as the first line of Chapter One did.

Springboard

Plan and write a story in five chapters, using the titles below. Don't forget the cliffhangers!

Chapter 1   A Step Too Far
Chapter 2   Waiting
Chapter 3   What a Find!
Chapter 4   Many Hands Make Light Work
Chapter 5   Just Rewards

ACTIVITY

Can you write a chapter that ends with one of these cliffhangers?

- When at last he woke, all he saw were stars in the purple sky above.
- There was only one thing for it: she would have to jump.
- Four more days of this!
- It was now or never. I took a deep breath and knocked on the door.

When you have finished, try to write the next chapter. Make sure the ending is a real page-turning cliffhanger.

PINK PIANO FOR SALE

Made especially for the Intergalactic Musical Instrument Exhibition this UNIQUE PINK PIANO is like no piano on Earth.

All offers considered – BUY IT NOW and discover its amazing musical effects on your next trip to the Red Planet!

Purple Sky Seen By All

Springboard

Now try a six-chapter book linking these chapter titles:

Chapter 1   The Pink Piano
Chapter 2   A Strange Teacher
Chapter 3   Making Excuses
Chapter 4   Music on Mars
Chapter 5   A Missing Note
Chapter 6   Home Again

JOINING THE DOTS

See how ingenious you can be at plotting a story that has to include certain, unconnected words at least once each.

These two story plans include each word from the list on the right. Both plans link the words into a storyline, but in a different order.

List of words
dandelion
camera
flew
pocket
soup

(Note: It is fine to use the words more than once!)

Plan 1

Mum asks you to pick **dandelion** leaves for salad. Pick a few – gets boring. Start blowing dandelion clocks. Seeds flew over next-door's fence. Old lady next door angry – doesn't want weeds in her veg patch – marches round to your mum. Mum invites old lady to stay to lunch. Old lady (Maud) delighted – says looks too good to eat: pulls camera out of pocket & photographs it before enjoying eating. Next day she pops round with home-grown leeks & potatoes. Digs recipe for leek & potato soup out of her pocket. You decide to cook it for dinner. You take photograph of finished soup. Ending: You, mum & old lady neighbour share more recipes & produce Community Cook Book – raises money for old people's drop-in centre (as old lady has said how lonely she is).

Plan 2

Outdoor picnic. Something looking like dandelion seed flew into cup of soup. Starts to grow. Shock! Amazement! Grab camera to photo as it grows rapidly. See woman walking by – struggling with her coat as seed begun growing in pocket. Same everywhere. Seeds growing in unlikely places. Young plants sprout legs & jump out, running in one direction. Everyone follows, huge space-ship descends, green creatures enter it. Disappears in space. People left dumbfounded – except central character. He/she has one last seedling: a miniature alien to keep as a pet/secret friend called…Dandelion!

(Note: this one is briefer; details need adding)

Note how one story is realistic, the other fantasy; but both started with the same list of words.

ACTIVITY

Choose a set of words from below. Write the words on bits of paper and shuffle them in any order.

- Let one or two words suggest the beginning of a story – a setting, character or event.
- Make brief notes as ideas come to you, perhaps using a spidergraph.
- Develop your notes into a simple story plan. These are the 'dots' that you will join up as you write your story.

Now 'join the dots' by thinking up an attention-grabbing start to your story and then carry on writing to the end.

Tip

There's no need to use full sentences in your story plan!

Set 1. bone   sneezed   window   suitcase   onions

Set 2. drum   valuable   spoon   swam   magnet

Set 3. helicopter   address   butterfly   sunset   danced   giraffe

Set 4. box   bald   mountain   enormous   circle   purple

Set 5. arrow   rainbow   owl   middle   castle   hungry   safe

Set 6. trip   lake   dragon   peaceful   party   tore   twenty   abandoned

Set 7. Saturday   damaged   lonely   ice   guitar   growl   danced   chicken

Tip

If there is a word that seems tricky to fit in, use a spidergraph and see what ideas you come up with.

Wild flower – where?
Worn in buttonhole

Dandelion and burdock fizzy drink

Dandelion: name of...pet? place? boat?

dandelion

Seed-head clock – children blowing seeds

Edible leaves – eaten in salads; also loved by rabbits and guinea pigs

The Dandelions: A rock band? Club? Secret society?

Springboard

- Think up more word lists to inspire 'join-the-dots' stories and swap them with your friends.
- Ask each family member to give you Đone word. Combine these into a list.
- Play a word-building game (such as Scrabble®) or complete a crossword. Then choose half a dozen words you have made for a word list.

STORY-MAPPING

Remember to decide early on from whose viewpoint you are telling the story.

Sometimes a writer's head can be buzzing with ideas. How do you decide which idea to develop from a number of different ones that all seem like good plot twists? Here's a way to sort out all your ideas and choose which ones to include and which to throw out. It's called a story-map.

A story-map makes it much easier to make sense of your ideas. Every time you make a decision your story changes direction. You end up writing a different story from what it would have been if you had made a different choice. Have a look at the story-map on the page opposite. A boy is setting off on holiday with his family. Where are they going and by what means of transport? Something unexpected is going to happen...

ACTIVITY

Follow the arrows from the top of the story-map opposite to choose a story-route. Write each choice on a sheet of paper. When you reach a question mark, use your imagination to make up the end of the story. When you have finished, you can draw up a storyboard to decide the order of events.

At this point, you can alter the order in which you describe events to the reader.

For example, you might begin your story with the boy knocking on a small cottage door. The cottage belongs to somebody whose phone number he rang earlier, when he found it in the glove compartment of the hire-car. (You can explain why the family hired a car later in the story.) It means that you can grab the reader's attention with an exciting part of the plot, drawing them into the story right from page one.

Springboard

Try finishing this story-map and see where it leads ...

IN THE JUNGLE
Two friends carrying backpacks are setting off along a jungle path.

One begins to shin up a creeper, like climbing a rope.

One sits down on a log for a drink.

The person looks down to see a snake is climbing up, too.

?

?

The backpack starts to shake violently.

THE HOLIDAY

Boy, sister, parents set off on holiday

to the seaside by car

children go surfing

find undersea treasure

?

meet a talking sea-creature

?

?

car breaks down

take a train instead

?

hire a car while theirs is fixed – find something curious in the glove compartment

a note mentioning a reward and a phone number

?

they ring the number and a squeaky voice replies

a camera with a half-used film

?

they have the film processed and see the picture of a long-lost relative

the film contains pictures of a robbery

?

?

abroad by plane

luggage goes missing

it arrives on next flight but something has been removed

they change plans and follow their luggage

arrive to find hotel closed down and boarded up

?

?

break in and camp there but so does someone else ...who? why?

local farmer takes pity on them and offers rooms

?

farmer appears to be using the premises for more than just farming...

farmer offers Dad a job and they decide to stay longer...

boy wants to go home and runs away

?

?

?

SUMMING UP

Planning characters, setting, plot, opening lines, viewpoint... what a lot of things an author has to weave together to create a story! The main thing – if you enjoy writing – is to stick at it. Keep practising. Here are some reminders.

Reminder checklist

Here are some things to remember when writing stories.

- Make sure first lines grab attention.
- Show rather than tell.
- Experiment with different voices – write in different characters.
- Use dialogue to break up narrative.
- Read aloud and rewrite to improve the flow.
- Use all five senses in description.
- Vary your sentence length to change pace.
- Tie up any loose ends before the close of your story.
- Create a happy ending – satisfying for the reader.
- End chapters with a page-turning cliff-hanger.
- Check and 'proof-read' your story:
  - Do all pronouns agree with their subjects?
  - Is your continuity of action accurate?
  - Have you overused certain words?
  - Have you checked spellings?
  - Is your use of tense consistent?

What next?

Now that your writing is finished, here are some things to do with it:

- Start a writers' club with like-minded friends. Read your stories to each other. Give and take helpful critiques (constructive critical comments on your writing). No author ever stops learning how to improve!

- Produce a short-story **anthology** with your friends, containing a story by each of you.

- Desk-top publish your stories – adding illustrations – on your computer. You could staple them together to create a whole library of your own books!

• Get together with friends to publish a magazine for other friends and family to enjoy.

• Look out for writing competitions to enter. These are often advertised in libraries and bookshops. Some appear on websites – but check who is running them first. Are they a well-established publisher or arts group? Do they have a junior section? Do they have a junior section? Are they free to enter? Check with an adult first.

Springboard 1

Try developing any of these ideas as stories:

Something appears... in the steam of the kettle... through the window... in the mirror... on the computer... or a presenter speaks to you from the TV screen... WHAT HAPPENS NEXT?

Springboard 2

A child goes to the aid of an old person who has fallen down. What happens next? Maybe the two find that they have something unlikely in common, such as odd socks or very elderly pet goldfish. Perhaps the old person gives their helper a reward - where does that lead them next?

Springboard 3

You find a ball which, when it bounces, does something magical – it always goes where you kick or throw it; it glows and hums and an alien emerges; or it bursts like a balloon and suddenly snow falls in summer? Think of a reason to explain the magical event. For example, snow might help penguins that are overheating in the local zoo.

How To Write

POEMS

Get to grips with rhyme!

Tips and techniques from a real poet

Now YOU can write:
- marvellous metaphors
- amazing alliteration
- rhythm and rhyme schemes

CONTENTS

ALL KINDS OF POEMS

People have been writing poems for a very long time. They were written in China 3000 years ago, for example. Famous poets include playwright William Shakespeare, who wrote poetry in the late 1500s. Roald Dahl's stories are familiar, but he also wrote books of poems, such as *Revolting Rhymes* and *Rhyme Stew*. Today, there are plenty of well-known children's poets, such as Michael Rosen and Roger McGough. Anyone can write a poem...including you!

What makes poetry different?

Poems and stories contain words, and both communicate with the reader. However, there are differences:

- Poems tend to be short and try to convey meaning with just a few words.
- Some stories are short, but many are thousands of words long.

- Poems are sometimes divided up into **verses**.
- Stories have **paragraphs** and **chapters**.

- Poems have a beat, or **rhythm**, and sometimes use **rhyme**.
- Stories don't!

- A poem can make a pattern or shape on the page.
- Stories are set out in rectangles of print.

What are poems about?

A poem can be about anything that you want to express yourself about.

- A poem can tell a story – or re-tell an existing one, such as *Little Red Riding Hood*.
- A poem can be about feelings...what it feels like to score a winning goal, or how you felt when your pet cat died.
- A poem can describe, for example, a sandy beach, autumn leaves falling or your street in the snow.
- A poem can be about a person, a creature or the weather.
- A poem can try to capture a particular moment in words.

Getting ready to write

You'll need a pen or pencil and a workbook – or lots of sheets of paper. Or perhaps you prefer to work on a computer. Wherever you work, you'll need a quiet place to gather together your thoughts.

Different kinds of poems

There are many different **genres** of poetry. Take a look at some of them.

Narrative poem

A long poem that tells a story is called a narrative poem. Famous narrative poems, such as *The Highwayman* by Alfred Noyes, tell stories using rhyme. A ballad is a short narrative poem with a **refrain** at the end of each verse.

Haiku

A traditional Japanese poem that has only three lines and 17 **syllables**.

Sonnet

A sonnet has 14 lines and follows a **rhyme scheme**. For example, in Shakespeare's sonnets, for the first 12 lines, every other line rhymes. The last two lines rhyme with each other.

Limerick

A limerick is a funny five-line poem. Most limericks are nonsense poems.

Free verse

Most poems have rules, but some poems ignore all the rules. They don't rhyme and they have lines of different lengths. This is called **free verse**.

GETTING IDEAS

Ideas are all around you! An idea for a poem (or even just a **phrase**) can arrive at any time, even in the middle of the night! Your dreams can be a source of ideas. Keep a notebook with you at all times, so that you can jot down ideas as they come. Here are some ways to keep the ideas flowing.

Imagination

Use your imagination. Think, for example, of a cottage where no one has lived for 10 years. Ask yourself questions about what's inside the building. If you take yourself from room to room in your mind, your imagination will begin to work.

Feelings

Let your feelings tell you what to write. Something might make you feel sad, happy, cross, bored or worried. Try to write down your feelings to set you on the road to poetry.

Memories

Think of a place you enjoyed visiting, or how you felt on your first day at school or when your favourite pet died. Or look at photographs of past events you remember. We all have memories and these can be turned into poems, too.

Senses

Use all your senses of sight, hearing, touch, taste and smell to help you. For example, hold a pebble, a feather or a leaf in your hand. Make notes about the object's texture, size, weight and colour. This will give you solid material with which to begin a poem. This sort of writing will be mostly descriptive.

Mindmapping

A mindmapping session means writing down everything you can about a particular subject. For instance, if you have decided to write a poem about the seaside, the playground or falling snow, then without thinking too deeply just let your pen loose and jot down in your notebook all the words and ideas that immediately come into your head. You can draw upon these notes when you compose a poem.

Automatic writing

Automatic writing means writing without stopping for a little while – maybe two, three or four minutes. Just write down anything that comes into your head, even if it's the same word over and over again or 'I don't know what to write'. Whatever you do, don't stop! Perhaps you will end up with seven or eight lines of writing. At first, what you have written may not seem to make any sense, but you may find a phrase, or even just a word, to get you started on a new poem.

Spidergram

Another way to get ideas flowing is with a spidergram. Write a word that represents the subject of your poem in the middle of a piece of paper. Then write down as many words connected to the first word as you can. This may lead you to ideas that you would never have thought of otherwise. For example, in this spidergram, the idea of 'winter' leads to thoughts of both 'cold' and 'heat'.

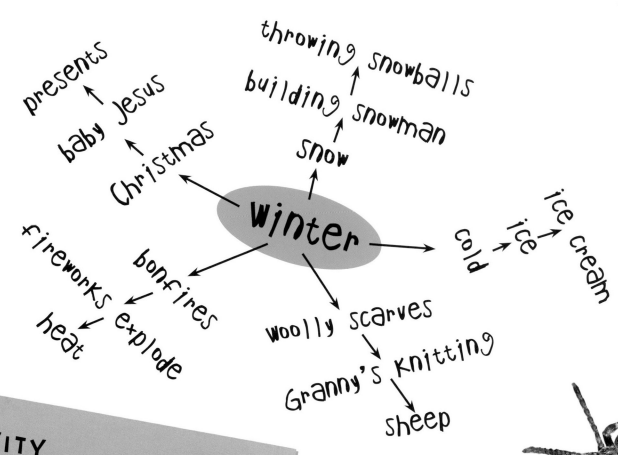

ACTIVITY

Make a spidergram. Draw a circle in the centre of a page in your notebook. Write a subject title (such as 'robin', 'tree' or 'my dog') in the circle. Now draw radiating lines (like spiders' legs). At the end of each line write down a word or brief note about the subject. Write a poem using some of the ideas from your spidergram. You may want to change the subject of the poem to one of the ideas on your spidergram's 'legs'.

Springboard

Take one of the words or a phrase from your spidergram and draw another spidergram based around it. Which new directions does it take you in? Are there any similarities with your first spidergram? Does it give you any useful words for a new poem?

RHYME AND RHYTHM

Many poems rhyme. It's a way of giving a poem structure and rhythm. It can give a poem a musical quality and it makes poetry easier to read aloud, too.

A sequence poem

A rhyming **sequence** poem is a great way to get started with writing poetry. A sequence poem tells you about things in the order that they happened. In the poem on the right, the days of the week are listed in the correct order, or sequence. Each day, from Monday to Sunday, has a two-line rhyming verse.

The words at the ends of each pair of lines rhyme ('down' and 'town'; 'ash' and 'crash', and so on). Lines that rhyme like this are called rhyming couplets.

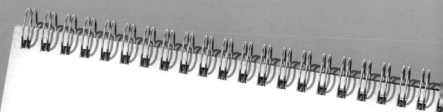

A WEEK OF WINTER WEATHER

* On Monday icy rain poured down and flooded drains all over town.

* Tuesday's gales bashed elm and ash, branches fell down with a crash.

* On Wednesday bursts of hail and sleet, no one walked along our street.

* Thursday stood out clear and calm, the sun was paler than my arm.

* Friday's frost that bit your ears was cold enough to freeze your tears.

* Saturday's sky was ghostly grey, we skated on the lake today.

* Christmas Eve was Sunday...and snow fell like foam across the land.

The week's weather

Mon 18th Dec	Tues 19th Dec	Wed 20th Dec	Thurs 21st Dec	Fri 22nd Dec	Sat 23rd Dec	Sun 24th Dec

ACTIVITY

Try writing a similar poem about a week of summer weather. First, write down all the words you can think of to describe different kinds of summer weather.

For example:

- sunshine
- hot
- cool breeze
- thunder

Choose seven of the different kinds of summer weather you wrote down, one for each day of the week.

Begin each verse with 'On…'.

The first verse could begin something like this:

On Monday, sunshine in cloudless blue skies

To complete the first rhyming couplet, write down words that rhyme with 'skies', such as 'sighs', 'lies', 'eyes', 'pies'…

By **drafting** and re-drafting the verse, you could end up with something like this:

On Monday, sun in cloudless skies,

I'm wearing shades to shield my eyes.

Springboard

Try writing a sequence poem based on one of the following themes:

- the seasons
- the months of the year
- numbers from one to ten

Dictionary

Tip

A rhyming dictionary is helpful if you are stuck for a rhyme.

When you have finished, read the verse aloud. Does it have rhythm? Does it make sense? Follow the same pattern and work your way through the rest of the sequence, from Monday to Sunday.

USING METAPHOR AND SIMILE

When you are writing poetry it can be very effective to describe something as if it is another thing that it reminds you of. This is called a **metaphor**. It is a picture in words – a 'word picture'. For example, 'the wind is a roaring lion' is a metaphor. The poet imagines that the wind is a roaring lion. He creates a picture of a roaring lion in our heads. In the poem below, each verse is a metaphor for the sun.

The Sun is an orange dinghy
    sailing across a calm sea.

It is a gold coin
    dropped down a drain in Heaven.

The Sun is a yellow beach ball
    kicked high into the summer sky.

It is a red thumbprint
    on a sheet of pale blue paper.

The Sun is a milk bottle's gold top
    floating in a puddle.

*In this poem the second line in each verse is **indented**.*

Springboard

Look at trees, or at pictures of trees in books. Write a simple metaphor poem about trees. Keep the lines short.

'Trees are gigantic gnarled hands.
Trees are huge mushrooms.
Trees are brains on spine stalks.
Trees are...
Trees are...'

ACTIVITY

Write a poem about the Moon using metaphor. In your notebook, make simple sketches of the Moon. It could be a full circle, a half circle or a crescent. Now ask yourself, what does the Moon remind you of?

A banana?
A table tennis ball?
A round cheese?
A silver brooch?
A sad face?
A smile?

List as many as you can.

Select from your list to compose verse 1. You could begin like this:

The Moon is a silver brooch

So far, so good. Can you 'extend' (continue) the metaphor? Remember, the Moon's background is the night sky, or Space.

Verse 1 could now develop like this:

The Moon is a silver brooch
on an ink-black, velvet gown

The 'ink-black, velvet gown' is a metaphor for the night sky.

Can you compose another verse – or even finish the poem?

Simile

Similes are similar to metaphors. They compare two things to make a word picture, using the word 'as' or 'like'. 'My love is like a red, red rose' and 'as strong as an ox' are two well-known similes.

ACTIVITY

Write a poem about feelings using similes. Write down some word pictures to describe how you feel about the things below.

Homework is like...
(a swirling black hole with no end in sight?).

Sunday is like...
(being free as a seabird gliding high above the ocean?).

and then...

My computer is like...
Feeling sad is like...
Having no pocket money is like...
Swimming in the pool is like...
The number 8 looks like...
The stars in the night sky are like...

Springboard

Write a poem using similes that contain the word 'as'. Well-known ones include 'as good as gold' and 'as white as a sheet'. Can you invent some new ones?

HAVING A LAUGH

Not all poetry is serious! Poems that make you laugh are fun to write. However, something that sounds comic in your head may not be so amusing when it's written down. When you've composed a funny poem, it's important to read it aloud to see if it makes not only you laugh, but your friends and family, too.

Here lies
Acker Abercrombie,
crazy name,
crazy zombie.
Slight scary,
rather rude,
he walks at midnight
in the nude.

Limericks

Limericks are humorous poems. They have their own rules.

> There was a young lady from Deal
> Who threw food around at each meal.
>   With manners so bad
>   She angered her Dad
> And made her poor Mum shout and squeal.

A limerick has five lines.

Lines 1, 2 and 5 rhyme. These lines have eight syllables.

The shorter lines (lines 3 and 4) rhyme with each other. These lines have five or six syllables.

ACTIVITY

See if you can write a limerick. Begin with an eight-syllable line, such as:
'There once was a girl with red eyes...'

Springboard

Here is the last line (line 5) of a limerick. Can you make up the previous four lines?

'Then slipped up and fell down the drain.'

Epitaphs

An epitaph is a short verse carved on a headstone, in memory of a person who has died. It usually says something about the dead person's character, habits or how they died. Epitaphs are usually serious; however, they can also be humorous.

Read the epitaph to the left and note the use of **alliteration** (words beginning with the same sound) to create a funny name. Also look at the pattern of each verse. By reading the epitaph aloud you will be able to 'hear' the rhymes properly.

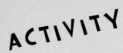

ACTIVITY

Write a four-line, rhyming epitaph for one (or more!) of the following:

Dracula
A grizzly bear
Sleeping Beauty
Bucktooth Bill
Monica Moody of Monterey

Clerihew

In the 1800s, an English novelist named Edmund Clerihew Bentley invented a new kind of poem. It was a funny, four-line rhyming poem about a person. The rules for a clerihew are simple.

ACTIVITY

Write a clerihew about yourself. Begin by writing your name. That's line 1 finished! Easy! Make a list of words that rhyme with your name. Think of something to say about yourself and write line 2. Now write lines 3 and 4.

The first line is the person's name.

→ Mrs. Cynthia Splat
→ owned a black and white cat.
→ They flew through the air
→ on a jet-propelled chair!

There are four lines consisting of two rhyming couplets.

The other lines can be any length.

The funnier and sillier the poem, the better.

TIP

If it's hard to find a rhyme for your surname, can you find one for your first or middle name – or for your nickname, if you have one?

SNAPSHOT POEMS

You can create a poem by using your eyes as a camera. Look closely at something, such as a wooden bench in the school playground, or a picture of an animal in a book – and take a snapshot with your eyes! Write down what you see.

A good way to turn your snapshot into poetry is to write a haiku. Haiku poems are snapshots and are very short.

A haiku poem has rules:

- It has three lines.
- Line 1 has five syllables.
- Line 2 has seven syllables.
- Line 3 has five syllables.
- It doesn't rhyme!

Here is a haiku poem about a fox:

Slinks to the wood's edge
and, with one paw raised, surveys
the open meadows.

What is a syllable?

A syllable is a separate sound (or part) within a word.
'Butterfly' has three syllables (or sounds): 'but–ter–fly'.
'Cat' has one syllable.
'River' has two syllables: 'ri–ver'.

Count the syllables in the haiku about the fox. Does it have the five – seven – five pattern of syllables?

Did you know?

Haiku is a Japanese form of poetry. Haikus are sometimes called 'one-breath' poems as they are short enough to be spoken between one breath and the next.

Springboard

Write a sequence of five haiku poems about pets. Draw up a list of pets (such as cat, dog, stick insect, lizard, hamster, pony, goldfish). Select five. Draft your haiku poems. Remember to use your eyes as a camera!

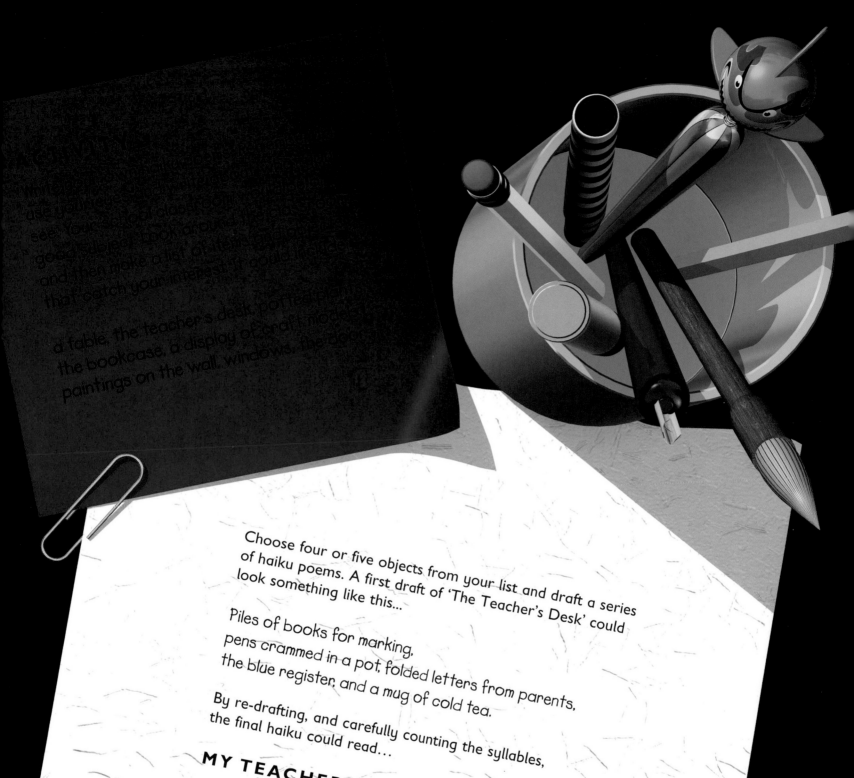

ACTIVITY

...use your... s... close... r... classroom... th...
see. You... should... close... around...
good... look... look around...
and then make a list of... item... that...
that catch your interest... could in... e...

a table, the teacher's desk, portrait painting,
the bookcase, a display of craft models,
paintings on the wall, windows, the door...

Choose four or five objects from your list and draft a series of haiku poems. A first draft of 'The Teacher's Desk' could look something like this...

Piles of books for marking,
pens crammed in a pot, folded letters from parents,
the blue register, and a mug of cold tea.

By re-drafting, and carefully counting the syllables, the final haiku could read...

MY TEACHER'S DESK

Books left for marking,
pens crammed in a pot, letters,   **(five syllables)**
cracked mug of cold tea.   **(seven syllables)**
                                    (five syllables)

See if you can complete a sequence of haiku based on other classroom objects.

A MEMORY POEM

Poets often write about things that they remember from the past. Thomas Hood, an English poet who lived in the 1800s, wrote a poem called 'I remember…'. It begins:

> I remember, I remember,
> The house where I was born.
> The little window where the sun
> Came peeping in at morn…

Automatic writing

One way to get ideas for writing a memory poem is to just let your pen run across the page and write down everything you can remember. This is known as automatic writing. Authors often do this when trying to write down their memories.

Here is a verse from a poem about a child visiting an aunt's house:

Remembering a house

Try some automatic writing. Can you remember a house you visited when you were younger? Perhaps it was your Gran's house. Perhaps it was an unusual house. What do you remember about it? When you have got some ideas down on paper, begin to extract items from your writing and shape your memory poem.

Add a refrain

What was the thing you enjoyed most at the house? (At Aunt Lil's, it was her 'delicious doughnuts'.) Add your favourite thing to the end of your verse to act like a **chorus** or refrain. Can you write a second and third verse? Don't forget to repeat the chorus!

AT AUNT LIL'S HOUSE

I remember
going to Aunt Lil's house.
There was my uncle's gold watch,
a blazing fire, doorsteps of toast,
her yellow canary, two kittens,
and on the stairs…a ghost,
…and
delicious
doughnuts!

When you write free verse, it gives you the chance to make your poem into an interesting shape on the page.

No rhyme this time!

Use rhyme if you wish or create a free-verse poem with no rhyme. For example:

"Who," questioned my mother,
"helped themselves to the new loaf?"
But my two friends and I
looked at her
and shrugged.

Springboard

What's the very first thing you can remember? Write it down, trying to create the scene...
Where was it?
What happened there?
What did you see or hear?
Was anyone else there?
Was there a particular smell?

See if you can write a free-verse poem about your first memory.

A sense of time

You can use your senses to remember things that have happened in the past. Take yourself back to an event and try to remember the sights, sounds and smells. Can you remember any tastes or how things felt to the touch?

ACTIVITY

Try writing a poem based on memories of just one of your senses. For example, what pleasant smells can you remember? List as many smells as you can. Then draft a poem. For example:

The pleasant smell
of dinner cooking in the kitchen
on Christmas Day morning

The pleasnt smell
of shampoo and bubbles
when I wallow in a hot bath

The pleasant smell of...

Tip

Don't worry about spelling, punctuation or neat handwriting when you are doing automatic writing. Just let your pen write!

47

A PERSONA POEM

A persona poem is one written with the 'voice' of someone (or something) else. The poet writes from the viewpoint of another being. The actual author of the poem below could be anyone – adult, child, boy or girl – but it is written as if the boy in the poem is speaking. He is telling you his story.

Some of the words rhyme, but not in a regular pattern.

I like Emma
but I don't know
if she likes me.
All the boys
think I'm a fool.

I wait beside the school gate
at half-past three
trying to keep my cool.
Emma walks past
shaking her long hair free,
laughs with her friends
and drifts off home for tea.

Using imagination

This is a love poem. The boy likes Emma, but she is two years older and perhaps doesn't even notice him. It is also a persona poem. The author imagines being the boy and writes about what the boy is thinking.

Different rhymes

'I Like Emma' has rhymes. If you read the poem aloud you will hear the rhyming words. The rhymes do not occur regularly, such as in every other line. They jump about, popping up every few lines or so.

Animals and objects

Persona poems can express the imagined thoughts of creatures (a mouse or a shark, for instance). They can also voice the 'thoughts' of objects, such as a pebble on the beach, the stars or a teapot.

Springboard

Write a persona poem that involves awful weather conditions. For example, write about someone lost in a blizzard. Keep the lines short and the feeling tense. Remember to write from the lost person's point of view. Don't use rhymes or verses. Just concentrate on making the poem powerful.

Here's an example of a persona poem about a pet cat.

THE CAT'S POEM
Out in the back garden
I find a warm, wind-free spot
and love to curl up and sleep.
I dream about mice...

ACTIVITY

Write a persona poem from the viewpoint of a pebble on a beach. Write in the first person ('I') and describe the pebble's experiences. For example, how does it feel to be rolled by the tide, worn smooth by the waves or thrown into the sea by a child? An unusual ending might be the pebble being taken home as a souvenir.

Redrafting the poem and adding some irregular rhymes improves it.

THE TABBY CAT'S POEM
Out here in the back garden
it's great to find a sheltered spot
where I can curl up in the sun.
This is fun!
Yawn!
I like it when it's hot.
I dream about mice
a lot...

Tip

It helps to write your poem in the first person ('I'). That way it sounds as if the pet is 'saying' the poem.

THE SOUNDS OF WORDS

It's important to think about the sounds of the words you choose for your poems because they affect the rhythm and the rhyme, too (if it is a rhyming poem). The sounds of the words also make a difference because poems are intended for reading aloud.

Snap, crackle, pop!

You can make good use of words that sound like their meanings. This is called **onomatopoeia**. For example, 'cuckoo' actually sounds like a cuckoo's call! When you say the word 'sizzle' you can almost hear the sausages sizzling in the pan! This poem contains onomatopoeic words. Read the poem aloud. Can you hear them?

THE WATERFALL

Over rugged rocks
the waterfall tumbles,
and rumbles.

In winter
it gasps, groans,
and grumbles.

But in summer it's quiet.
It just whispers
and mumbles.

How now brown cow

It can be very effective to group words with similar vowel sounds together. This is called **assonance**. It gives words more emphasis. For example:

A black cat pads across the patio
leaving small paw prints in the snow.

Can you spot an example of assonance in line 2?

The words 'black', 'cat', 'pads' and 'patio' all have the same vowel sound.

Springboard

Think about your bedroom late at night. Write a poem about all the sounds you might hear as you lie in bed. There will be sounds in the bedroom itself (radiators gurgling, wardrobe doors creaking, the duvet rustling), sounds from the rest of the house (the toilet flushing, parents' muffled voices, stairs creaking), and sounds from outside (footsteps clicking on the pavement, a motorbike roaring, branches tapping at the window, rain pattering).

ACTIVITY

In your notebook, write down as many words as you can for the following:

- Words to describe loud noises, such as 'bang!' or 'whack!'.
- Words to describe quiet sounds, such as 'creak' or 'whisper'.

Compose a poem about sounds you hear at school. Write verse 1 about loud noises. Include some of the words from your notebook. For example:

'The screams and squeals of children
in the playground at morning break'

Write verse 2 about the quiet noises you would hear. For example:

'The ping and drip of wet raincoats
in the damp cloakroom on a dull winter's day'

Animal noises

The words we use to describe the sounds animals make are onomatopoeic: the roar of a lion, a dog's bark. Can you add the appropriate 'sound' words to this list?

the hiss of a snake
the.......of a cat
the.......of an owl
the.......of a mouse
the.......of a sheep
the.......of a seagull
the.......of a horse
the.......of sparrows

Can you think of appropriate noises for other, more unusual, animals? Be as inventive as you like – the squelch of a squid or the rumble of an ox, for example.

Words, words, words

It can be very effective to include in your poems groups of words that begin with the same letter. This is called alliteration. Different letter-sounds create different effects. For example, soft sounds, such as 'w' or 'l' can be used to create an atmosphere of gentleness, while hard sounds, such as 'p' or 'ch' have the opposite effect.

Slowly, the silent snake slips across silver sand.
Clumsy Clive clatters by in a clapped-out car.

Tip

Newspaper articles often have alliterative titles to grab the reader's attention. You can do the same by giving your poems snappy, alliterative titles.

'S' creates a sinister atmosphere – and reminds the reader that 's-s-s' is the sound the snake makes.

'Cl' makes a clattering sound – just like the car.

AN IMAGINATIVE POEM

All writers try to use their imagination to invent people, places and events. You may have never visited an old, deserted house but it is possible to imagine what it must be like there. This poem imagines and describes the furniture and objects you might find inside an old house.

The verse has its own special pattern. Note the indented lines.

In the hall
cobwebs hang from the crumbling ceiling,
antlered hat-stand carved from oak,
crimson carpet's tattered and torn,
and dust in the air makes you choke.
  Chilly,
  icy mansion.
  Dark,
  deserted place.

There are rhymes at the end of lines 3 and 5.

The final four short lines act as a chorus, or refrain.

ACTIVITY

Make an imaginary tour of a deserted mansion. List as many rooms as possible that you would find there. Don't forget the attic, the cellar, the library and pantry. Now let your mind 'walk' from room to room, imagining all the things you'd see, hear and touch (and smell!) in the mansion.

Write a verse for the poem. Begin by choosing a room, for example, the kitchen. Ask yourself what's there? Close your eyes and really see that kitchen. Don't forget to add the chorus or refrain at the end of your verse. You could compose a longer poem by taking a different room as the subject for each verse.

Stretch your imagination

You can use your imagination to bring to mind things that can't actually be there in front of you. For instance, you could try to imagine what it's like to be on a distant star, or to be a creature that lives in an ice cave. Try using your imagination to answer these questions:

- What's behind the curtain on the school hall stage?

- Who lives inside a hollow tree? (Not an owl or a squirrel!)

- Where do cats go at midnight?

- What happens when the clock strikes 13?

Springboard

It's the end of the Christmas holiday. You turn up at the school playground ...a day early! Of course, there are no children to be seen. Try to imagine what it would be like. 'Paint' the playground scene in words, and don't forget to include the weather (snow on the tarmac?), the silence, pieces of litter blowing around and any creatures you might see (birds, a stray cat?). Turn your writing into a free-verse poem.

ACTIVITY

Look closely at a simple, everyday object, such as a pencil. It is straight, thin and smooth. Now try to imagine it is something else. It could be a rocket travelling to Mars, or the fossilized stem of a prehistoric plant. Concentrate hard on that object. Can you imagine other things it could be?

Tip

Avoid repeating words (except in the chorus!) to keep your writing fresh and interesting. Use a **thesaurus** to help you find words that have similar meanings. For example, you could say 'gloomy' instead of 'dark'. You can find a thesaurus on the Internet or in book form.

Springboard

It's your eccentric great aunt's birthday party and lots of relatives have been invited – including you! It's going to be a wild party! Imagine what happens. Describe some of the guests, the games and the food. Write a three-verse poem, each verse being about a different aspect of the party.

RIDDLES

A riddle is a 'puzzle-me-out' poem about a person, animal or object. The idea is to give clues and the reader has to guess the answer. Riddles are a very old type of poetry. The Anglo-Saxons used to recite them around log fires more than a thousand years ago! Riddles are usually written in the first person 'I', as if they are speaking to you.

ACTIVITY

Have a go at writing a riddle. Choose a subject from the list below or think of one of your own. It could be a person, an animal or an object. Make a list of things about your chosen subject. Then use your list to write your clues.

The sea
A cat
Ripe apples hanging on a tree
A chair
Your favourite cartoon character
Your fingers

What am I?

I am as flat as a football field.
I have legs, but I never walk.
I don't speak although I can squeak.
People sit around me and eat hot dogs or ice-cream but never think of feeding me!
What am I?

Answer: a table!

Tip

If you work on a computer, you can try out lots of versions of your riddle until you get the right one. Then email it to your friends and see who can figure it out!

Descriptive riddle

Some riddles are more descriptive. They tell you more than just the clues you need to solve them.

I am like an open, yellow eye at night,
never blinking, always staring down
from the limitless darkness.
And so cold. Oh, I'm so cold!
And lifeless! It's true!

Visitors came to see me
but they didn't stay long
before zooming off as fast as
they could.
No wonder I look so sad.
Alone and sad
in this limitless darkness.

Answer: the moon

Acrostic riddles

An acrostic is a poem in which the first letter of each line forms a word when read vertically. Have a go at composing an acrostic riddle. Spell out the letters of the answer to your riddle down the page, like this:

S
N
A
K
E

Use the initial letters (the acrostic) to write your clues.

Slowly I wriggle through grass.

Now I...

After...

Of course, the answer to the acrostic riddle is easy. It's written down the page! But it is a fun way of writing.

Springboard

Acrostic poems don't have to be riddles. Try writing an acrostic in another poetic form, such as a haiku, or an epitaph – spelling out the name of the subject vertically.

TO RHYME OR NOT TO RHYME?

Your poems don't have to rhyme, but it can be easier to give them a structure if they do. Rhyming gives poems a 'musical' quality. That's why songs contain rhymes! Rhymes also make poems easier to read and to remember if you want to learn them by heart.

Rhyming patterns

One way to make poems rhyme is to use rhyming couplets. The first line rhymes with the second, the third line with the fourth, and so on.

Another kind of rhyme is a triplet. In a triplet there are three rhymes in a three-line verse. This poem is a persona poem about a dog, and is written as a triplet:

> My barking drives them up the wall.
> I chew the carpet in the hall.
> I love to chase a bouncing ball.

Tip

When you write rhyming poetry, keep asking yourself if you have found the right rhyme. Read your poem aloud. Does it sound good – or really bad? If it's not right, look for a better rhyme.

ACTIVITY

Write a persona poem in triplets. It could be about a pet, such as a cat or rabbit, or about a person or an object. In your notebook, write down all the things a rabbit, for example, might do.

> Sleeps in a straw bed.
> Nibbles carrots.
> Eats lettuce and dried food.
> Hops.
> Has soft fur.
> Has long, floppy ears.
> Lives in a hutch.

Think of some one-syllable words that rhyme with a word in your notes. For example, find rhymes for 'hops' (slops, stops, pops, tops). Draft and then write the first verse. Can you write another two verses using different word rhymes?

Different patterns

Another rhyme pattern is a four-line verse with the second and fourth lines rhyming. This rhyme pattern is known as ABCB.

Andrew Flag plays football,   (A)
Beth swings from the bars.   (B)
Abbi eats an apple,   (C)
And Steve is seeing stars.   (B)

Try writing a verse with an ABCB pattern. It could be a second verse to the poem above, or use your own ideas.

Non-rhyming verse

A poem that doesn't rhyme and has lines and verses of different lengths is known as free verse. Sometimes it is good to write without having to think about rules or restrictions. It's a chance to express your feelings freely or to describe what you see.

A HARD WINTER

    Not a twig stirs.
    The frost-bitten garden
    huddles beneath
    a heaped duvet of snow.
    Pond,
    tree,
    sky
    and street
    are granite with cold.

ACTIVITY

Try your hand at a free-verse poem about a holiday. Draft it in your notebook. Ask yourself these questions:

Where did you go?
What did you see?
What did you like about the place?
Did anything memorable happen?
Did you bring home a souvenir?

Write some lines of poetry. Think about where each line should end. Keep reading your work aloud and listen to the rhythm of the words. This will help you to see where to put the line breaks.

Springboard

Try out different rhyme patterns. How about a four-line verse with rhymes in lines 1 and 2 and different rhymes for lines 3 and 4? (AABB) It could even be a five-line verse with rhymes in lines 1, 3, and 5. (ABACA) It's interesting to experiment with rhyme. Try creating your own rhyming patterns.

SUMMING UP

We have learned a great deal about writing poems. Everything from using rhymes (such as couplets and triplets) and different patterns on the page, to sequence poems and metaphor poems (word pictures).

Rules

We discovered that poems have rules. Many rules are there to help the poet. They are useful. However, it is possible to break the rules, if you wish. You can create your own free-verse poems, and no one can say to you, "Hey, don't do that!"

Drafting

We also mentioned drafting. It would be wonderful if a poem 'came out right' first time. We'd all like that. Occasionally it happens, but usually the poet needs to make notes (or lists), then write and re-write (draft). This helps you to finish the poem properly, to give it polish.

Poems, like songs or hymns, are for saying aloud. If you recite your poem (or poems) to a group or class it helps if you do this:

- Keep your head up.
- Read slowly and clearly.
- Add expression to your voice.
- Make eye contact with the listeners.
- Add hand actions to emphasize the words.

Keep your poems and make a book of them. Perhaps one day you could be a published poet. You just never know!

Presentation

It's good to see a poem properly finished. This means presenting it really neatly and carefully. Think about how your poem will look on the page (or computer screen). This is the poem's pattern. By using a computer you can achieve fantastic lay-out effects.

Pictures

Illustrations (artworks) always help to make a page really attractive. If you don't want to draw, try adding simple designs or borders. Colour them carefully. And there's always Clip Art from your computer, too.

Make notes about everything you might do on a visit to the swimming pool. This is your first draft (see below). Begin to put the notes in the correct order as they happened. For example: Pay at the desk in the entrance. Walk through the swing doors. Go to the changing rooms... and so on, until you leave the swimming pool. This is the second draft. Write out the sequence, giving it a special pattern (or shape) on the page. This is the third, and final, draft - you have a poem!

Make a list of all the objects and items you might find in an attic. (For example: old books, a framed painting, pair of shoes, dolls' house.) Now arrange the list in the shape of a staircase (or ladder) ascending to the attic. You can link the words in the list with words and phrases, such as 'and', 'as well' or 'not forgetting'.

First draft

Pay at the desk
Get changed
Get in the pool
Swim for 20 minutes
Get changed again

Second draft

Pay at the desk
Walk through the swing doors
Go to the changing rooms
Dash barefoot to the pool
Clamp on the goggles
Plunge into the warm water
Float on my back
Swim on my front
Swim under the water
Leave the pool
Drip, drip, drip....

Third draft

Pay at the desk
doors   Walk through the swing
rooms   Go to the changing
pool   Dash barefoot to the
         Clamp on the goggles
water   Plunge into the warm
Float on my back
Swim on my front
Swim under the water
Leave the pool
Drip,
    drip,
        drip...

Springboard 3

How many rhyming words can you think of for these words? Make the lists as long as possible.

hair   door   sky   under   tree

Now choose one of your lists as the starting point for a poem.

Tips and techniques from a real writer

How To Write

REPORTS

Get top marks for technique!

Now YOU can write:

- reports and articles
- riveting recounts
- perfectly planned projects

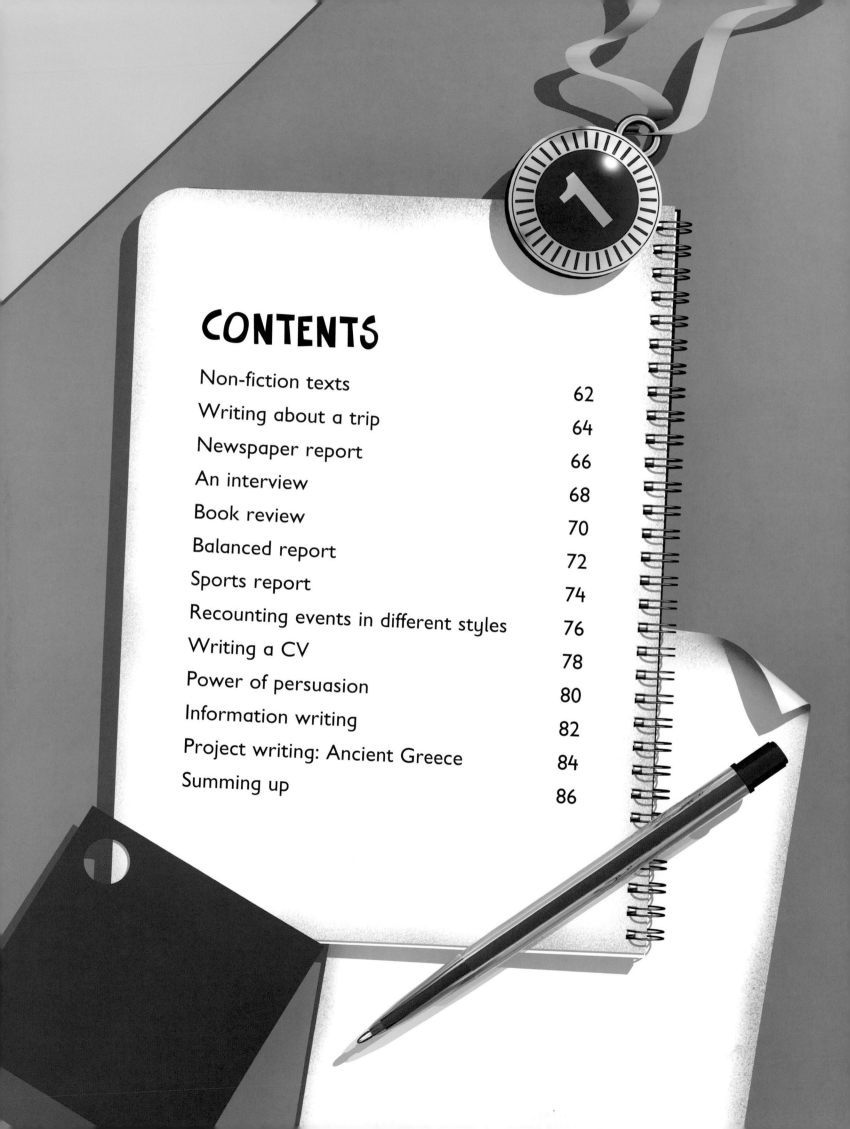

CONTENTS

NON-FICTION TEXTS

When you write about yourself and the world around you, giving information, facts and, sometimes, personal opinions, you are writing non-fiction. There are all sorts of non-fiction texts. A newspaper report, a **CV**, a **review**, a **recount** of a holiday, a balanced argument and a project on the rainforest are all examples of non-fiction writing.

Purpose

The words you use and how you present your writing depends on what sort of non-fiction you want to write. Are you writing for a class newspaper? Then you need a catchy **headline**. Are you doing a project about the Ancient Greeks? Then you need to organize the information under **subheadings**, with each subheading introducing a new aspect of the topic.

Audience

Who will be reading what you've written? If your writing is intended for your friends, then you can use language that they are familiar with and word **contractions**, such as 'doesn't' and 'won't'. If your writing is for your teacher or someone you don't know, then you should use formal language – 'will not', for example – and avoid words like 'brilliant' and 'cool'.

A class diary is an example of a non-fiction text.

glue stick

Class 6 Diary
My birthday treat
by Leonie Smith

June 10th
For my birthday, my dad took me to visit Zone Studios on Saturday. Galaxy Gorgons, my favourite film, was made here.
 In the first building were the sets from some of the scenes. In one corner, we even saw the gorgons' spaceship! We entered a workshop where people were working on a model of a monstrous one-eyed fish. Maybe this character will star in the next Galaxy film!

Then we went into the props and costumes department – and saw the necklace with extra-sensory powers! Finally, we passed through a room full of computers where people were playing with on-screen graphics. This was my best ever birthday treat.

THEY CAME FROM OUTER SPACE...

The Galaxy Gorgons

STARRING

Researching

As non-fiction writing is about facts, you need to research your information. Talk to people with knowledge or experience, and use books or the Internet. Keep a notebook of interesting facts that you can use in later writing. Make sketches, too, if you like.

Boa constrictor eats prey live

Largest land animal = African elephant

Teddy bear named after President Roosevelt

Singapore = city of lions

Tip

Nobody can get it all right the first time they write. You need to plan and prepare an outline, either as a diagram or chart, or as a list, before writing.

Once you've written a **draft**, you may want to use a word-processing program to move **paragraphs** around or to do a **spell-check**.

Here are some good websites to use when you are doing your research:

www.thebritishmuseum.ac.uk

www.bbc.co.uk/cbbc/

www.enchantedlearning.com

Did you know?

Leonardo da Vinci filled his notebooks with sketches of all sorts of things: a bird's wing, devices to make water flow, hats. He also did mirror writing, going backwards across the page to form a mirror image of his normal writing.

WRITING ABOUT A TRIP

A piece of writing that retells events in the order in which they happened is called a recount. Suppose you've been on a school trip and your teacher has asked you to write about it. The best way to do this is to describe the events as you experienced them.

Starting to write

Present the events in chronological order. Describe briefly the place you were visiting so that the reader can get a flavour of it. Since you were the person who experienced everything, write from your point of view, either using the pronoun 'I' or, if you were with your class or friends, 'we'. Make your writing interesting by adding your own observations and feelings.

Which tense?

You should write in the past tense because you are describing events that have already taken place.

All in order

Before you start, it's helpful to draw a timeline. Write down the events of the trip in the order that they happened from start to finish. You only need to write key words or abbreviations that will help you to write your recount.

Useful words to use that show the sequence of events:

- First
- Next
- Then
- Shortly after
- Later
- Finally

Start with a sentence that sets the scene.

Each paragraph explains a different event in chronological order.

Try to include some unusual facts to keep your reader interested.

Notes for trip to Miramar
Guide – Tunnel – Reefs (coral) –
Coast (sharks!) Shipwreck – Dangerzone
(snakes) – Talk

Give your recount a title that tells the reader what it is about.

Break the text into paragraphs to make it easier to read.

Our trip to the aquatic life centre

Today we visited the Miramar Aquatic Life Centre. Our coach pulled up just as it was opening. Inside, our guide was waiting for us. We followed him down into a transparent tunnel, with the sea all around. There were real-life fish swimming right up to us.

First, we visited the Reefs Sanctuary, with hundreds of rainbow-coloured fish darting in and out of bits of red and pink coral. After that, we moved on to the Coast Sanctuary, which had huge stingrays, turtles, sharks and even a shipwreck. One shark came swimming right up to me. I had never been face to face with a shark before and I was so glad that I was safe in the tunnel, away from its huge teeth.

Next, we visited the Dangerzone. It had sea snakes and gigantic jellyfish.

After lunch, we listened to a talk on some of the fish we'd seen. It was really interesting. Did you know that the jellyfish has no brain?

By the time we'd finished we were tired and ready for the ride home, but it had been a great day!

After retelling the events, end with a closing statement

Springboard

Write a recount of a family outing or a trip to a museum. Begin by making a timeline of the main events. Don't forget to use some time-sequencing words (first, next and so on).

NEWSPAPER REPORT

Newspaper reports have to grab the reader's attention. They need punchy headlines and a gripping first few lines to make sure that you read on. News stories cover everything from world events to lost puppies. In the same way, you can turn anything exciting or unusual that happens to you into a news report.

News style

Flip through some newspaper **articles** and you'll see that they have things in common:

The headline (title) is set in large type. It consists of a few words only – just enough to catch the reader's eye.

the daily news

WALKING SHARK

Scientists discover a shark in the coral reefs off Indonesia that can walk on its fins

By Shah Kattak

A team of scientists has discovered many new species of fish and coral around the islands of Indonesia – including a fish that can walk.

Legging it
The shark is just over a metre long, with a slender body. It uses its pectoral fins as 'legs' to walk along the sea floor in search of food. Sam Sebastian, a leading member of the team, said, "They're extraordinary animals that sort of walk on their fins. They spend a lot of time on the bottom looking for mussels and crabs."

Watch the birdie
The coastal area, known as Bird's Head, is home to more than 1200 species of fish and almost 600 types of coral.

The introduction is one or two sentences long and says what the article is about.

The name of the person who wrote the article is known as the byline.

The paragraphs are arranged under subheadings.

The text is broken into short paragraphs.

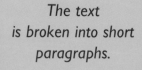

What to write?

Try writing a news report about something that has happened to you recently – the day your mum went to work in her slippers or when your school won a prize, for example. To catch the reader's eye you need an attention-grabbing headline. Make sure that it describes what your article is about. Use rhyme, **alliteration** or even puns – and keep it short!

Tackling the facts

A newspaper report describes what happened, who was involved, and when, how and where the event took place. Introduce the subject in the first paragraph. In the next paragraph build on what you have said, adding supporting facts, background information and **quotes**. Put less important details at the end of your article. For example, you might start with:

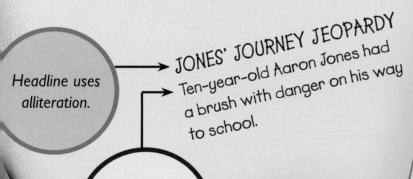

Headline uses alliteration.

JONES' JOURNEY JEOPARDY
Ten-year-old Aaron Jones had a brush with danger on his way to school.

First line makes you want to read on.

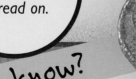

Did you know?

Newspapers have been around for a very long time. In Ancient Rome, the government kept its citizens informed of the latest developments in a war or the emperor's health through hand-written newssheets. These were placed in market squares where everyone could go and read them.

Tip
Use a computer to lay out your draft article in the style of a newspaper **column**. Vary the **fonts**, setting the headline in the largest font size and in **bold**. You'll need to **edit** your article to make it fit the column.

Writing style

Make your article exiting by varying your writing style.

- Follow a short sentence with a longer one.
- Use active verbs ('a storm lashed the town'), not passive ones ('the town was lashed by a storm').
- Introduce different points of view by using quotes from the people involved.
- **Divide** your writing into paragraphs of three or four sentences.
- Use **subheadings**.
- Break up your story with illustrations – either photos or drawings – and informative **captions**.

Springboard

Rewrite a nursery rhyme or fairy story as a newspaper report. Here's a headline to get you started: 'Eggs-hausting', says Humpty Dumpty.

AN INTERVIEW

An interview is a meeting with someone to ask them questions, either about themselves or on a special topic. The interviewer is the person who asks the questions and the interviewee is the person who answers them. The interviewer takes notes and then writes them up as a non-fiction text.

Tip

Always ask permission before you start your interview.

Who to interview?

You might wish to ask a local author about their writing, question your grandparents about life 50 years ago or even find out what your neighbours think about the shopping mall that's just opened nearby.

Preparing an interview

Make a list of questions. If you are interviewing people about their past life, your questions might be about the clothes they wore then, the music they enjoyed, their hobbies, or even how they got to school in the morning. Make sure you phrase your questions so that the person is encouraged to speak, and not to give 'yes' or 'no' answers.

Interview with Daz Dayman

Q. How did you feel when you got home?
A. v. happy & good 2 c my cats. Not v. much time 2 relax as next album 2 rcd.

Q. What do you think about a reunion?
A. wd like 2 c band m'bers agn

Q. What sort of music did you listen to?

A.

Q. What was it like...?

A.

Q. Tell me about...

A.

Abbreviate words as you write down answers.

Allow enough of a gap to write down your interviewee's answers.

ACTIVITY

Write down the questions on a notepad, leaving plenty of space between each one. Use this blank space to write down your interviewee's answers.

Tip

Take notes when you're writing down what your interviewee says, because you can't write as fast as they speak. Abbreviate words - just like you do when you're texting. Write 'lk' for 'like' and 'tdy' for 'today'. Leave out all small words, such as 'a' and 'the'. Use an ampersand (&) for 'and'.

Interviewing

Now that you've got a list of questions, set about finding the right person to answer them. If your project is about life in the 1950s, the best people to interview are grandparents and other older people. If you want to find out what people think about the new shopping mall, ask people who live in the area. Try to write down as much as you can so that you will be able to convey the character of your interviewee.

Writing up the interview

Begin your interview with an introduction, saying who the interviewee is and what the interview is about. Set out your interview like a playscript, with a new line for each speaker. Make the interview sound as if the interviewee is talking by using the actual words he or she used. Don't forget to replace your abbreviations with full words!

Begin a new line for each speaker.

Use initials to show who is speaking.

Include expressions that the interviewee uses, such as 'um', 'er' and 'oh', to make it sound as though they're speaking.

BEATLES' FAN ELLA EVANS TALKS TO HER NIECE, KIM, ABOUT GROWING UP IN THE 1960s.

KE: What did you like and dislike about school?

EE: My favourite lesson was geography. I loved learning about other countries. In those days, we didn't go on holiday abroad, so even learning about France seemed exotic! My least favourite subject was sewing. It would take me the whole lesson just to thread a needle!

KE: What did you want to be when you were my age?

EE: When I saw on television someone walking on the moon for the first time, it so impressed me that I wanted to be an astronaut.

KE: What sort of music did you like?

EE: My favourite music was rock-'n'-roll - oh, and anything by The Beatles.

Springboard

Make a list of questions you'd like to ask one of the following people:

- your favourite pop star
- a sporting hero
- Christopher Columbus
- a character from a book

BOOK REVIEW

A review is a report in which you give your opinion about, for example, a book, film, CD, concert, play or an exhibition.

Write a book review

How you write will depend on whether you are reviewing a **fiction** or non-fiction book. However, your review should always start with the title of the book, the name of the author and, if the book has pictures, the name of the illustrator or photographer.

Review a story or picture book

Tell the reader where the story takes place and describe the main characters. Write about the characters' relationships to each other. Are they school friends or did they meet through some strange coincidence? Describe the **plot** – but not in too much detail. Now give your opinion of the book. What do you like about the story? Is the plot convincing? Are the characters believable? Is it a book that you couldn't put down? If the book has illustrations, what did you like about them? Did they catch the mood?

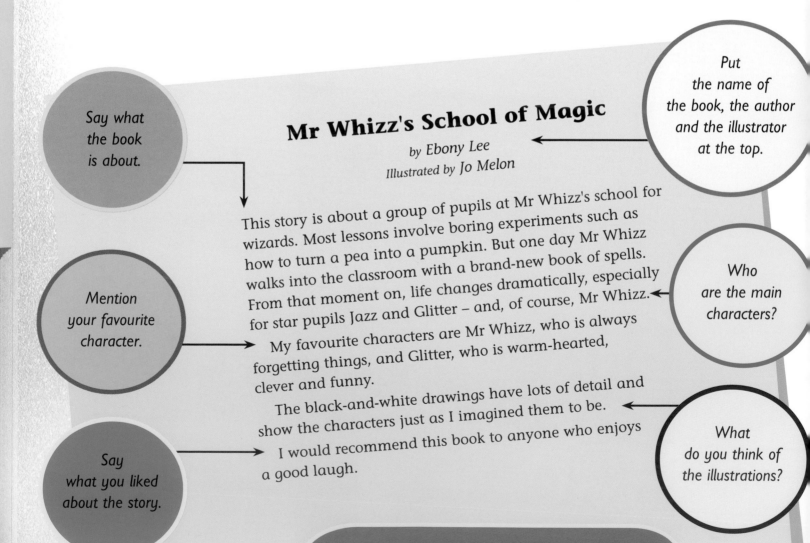

Say what the book is about.

Mention your favourite character.

Say what you liked about the story.

Mr Whizz's School of Magic

by Ebony Lee
Illustrated by Jo Melon

Put the name of the book, the author and the illustrator at the top.

This story is about a group of pupils at Mr Whizz's school for wizards. Most lessons involve boring experiments such as how to turn a pea into a pumpkin. But one day Mr Whizz walks into the classroom with a brand-new book of spells. From that moment on, life changes dramatically, especially for star pupils Jazz and Glitter – and, of course, Mr Whizz.

My favourite characters are Mr Whizz, who is always forgetting things, and Glitter, who is warm-hearted, clever and funny.

The black-and-white drawings have lots of detail and show the characters just as I imagined them to be.

I would recommend this book to anyone who enjoys a good laugh.

Who are the main characters?

What do you think of the illustrations?

Don't give away the ending. If your review has been successful, the reader will want to find out for themselves.

Review a non-fiction book

Reviewing a non-fiction book is a little different. Write a **summary** of the contents. Describe the way the book is organized. Does it have a **glossary** and an **index**? Does it have photos or diagrams to support the text? Now give your opinion of the book. Is it clearly written? Does it hold your interest and tell you what you wanted to know? Are the photographs eye-catching and informative? Do you know more about the topic after having read the book? Does the book make you want to read more about the topic?

Springboard

The best reviews are those that are written with enthusiasm. Review a film or a CD that you feel strongly about. This is important because if you write about something that you don't particularly like or dislike, what you write will also be half-hearted. If you find it boring, it'll be hard not to make your review sound dull, too.

Put the name of the book, the author and the photographer at the top.

Endangered Animals
By Joshua Squire
Photographs by Tammy Wayne

How are the contents organized?

Say what the book is about.

Describe photos and charts.

Mention any special features.

The book looks at animals, from every continent, that are in danger of extinction.

The book is divided into sections, one for each continent. Five types of animal – mammal, fish, bird, reptile and insect – are examined in each section. Under 'Australia' for example, you will find pages on the koala, saltwater crocodile, giant dragonfly, turquoise parrot and lungfish. The text is divided into subheadings that give facts about each animal and an explanation of why it is under threat.

The book has lots of large, really interesting photos. There's a map at the beginning of each section that shows where each animal comes from.

The book is well organized and clearly written, with an index so that you can find facts easily. It is so informative that it makes me want to find out more about the topic.

What did you like about the book?

BALANCED REPORT

A balanced report presents both sides of an argument and is usually made up of facts, or a mix of fact and opinion. Often the issue is **controversial**, with people either for or against it.

What's the purpose?

There are several reasons for writing a balanced report:

- To show that there are two sides to an argument.
- To give readers all the information they need to make up their minds about where they stand on an issue.
- To have all the facts in front of you before you take sides in a debate.

Facts, facts, facts

You'll need to research your topic thoroughly to find out the facts for and against an argument before setting out your report. Your research might include:

- Finding facts on the Internet or in your local library.
- Conducting a **survey** or **questionnaire**.
- Interviewing people.

Writing style

When you write up your report, use the present tense ('need' instead of 'needed') and use **impersonal language** ('it was found' instead of 'we found'...)

ACTIVITY

Try preparing a balanced report. There's a rumour flying around that a theme park is going to be built just outside your town. Some of your friends favour this proposal, others are against it. You're not sure where you stand so you need to gather all the facts. What arguments can you come up with, for and against?

Useful words

However • On the one hand/ On the other hand • Therefore • Then • To sum up • To conclude

Springboard

Choose one of these topics and produce a list of arguments for and against it. Try to have the same number of points in each column.

- Should school uniform be compulsory?
- Is tourism good for a country?
- Should zoos exist?
- Is reality TV entertainment?

Tip

Use bullet points for each new argument. This will make the information easier to read.

CLASS 6 REPORT

SHOULD THERE BE MORE SPORT IN THE SCHOOL DAY?

Class 6 reports on the arguments for and against more sport being introduced during the school day.

Begin with an opening statement to tell the reader what the report is about.

REMEMBER TO:

List 'for' and 'against' arguments in separate columns.

Write a point in favour of the argument and follow it with a point against.

Use impersonal language and the present tense.

FOR

- Children need more exercise, especially now that they are driven to school and spend free time watching TV and playing video games.

- Being overweight is a growing problem.

- There's too much time spent on subjects such as maths, so that children who are good at other things, like sport, lose out.

AGAINST

- It's not up to the school to provide more sport. Parents need to get their children to be more active.

- It would be better to give more time to teaching children about healthy eating instead.

- To cover all the subjects, the school day would have to be lengthened.

End your report with a statement summing up both arguments or stating which argument you agree with.

Place the 'for' and 'against' arguments alongside each other so that they roughly match up.

To sum up, after reading the arguments, Class 6 believes that it would be a good idea for children to play more sports during the school day.

SPORTS REPORT

Suppose that you've been asked to write about a school sports event – a swimming gala, the football finals, or a sports day event, such as the 100-metre race or even the egg-and-spoon race. How can you make your writing grab the reader's attention?

Starting to write

Here are some tips for spot-on sports reporting:

- Keep sentences short and avoid **explanatory clauses**. For example, instead of writing 'All eyes were on Hari, who, as well as being really popular, was the school's best sprinter', you could say 'All eyes were on Hari. He was the school's best sprinter. He was also really popular'.

- Use an **active voice** ('Ben pounded the ground'). A **passive voice** ('the ground was pounded by Ben'), will slow down your writing.

- Use **metaphors** and **similes** – 'Anya was a white streak in the distance', 'Misha raced like the wind'.

- Build mood. For example, describe the suspense before the race. Which of the entrants looked nervous/confident? Were the spectators noisy with excitement or hushed with suspense? You could also describe key moments of tension – the moment when Jay's dog slipped its collar one minute into the race and rushed along the track, almost tripping her up.

Springboard

Write a report about your school team's most recent match. (Choose any team sport, such as football or netball.) Write the report as if you are writing for a local newspaper and the team members are local sports stars. Include quotes from the team and from their manager, of course.

ACTIVITY

Choose a sport to write about. How are you going to present it? Are you going to start with the result, 'Anna wins by a whisker'? Or do you wish to write it as the event takes place, keeping your audience in suspense until the very end? If so, describe the sequence of events as they happen.

Organize your writing into short paragraphs to make it easier to read and hold the reader's interest.

Use adjectives, but use them sparingly as too many will slow down the impact of your writing.

United win

by Joshua Squire

A brilliant strike by newcomer Fernando saves the day for reigning champions, United. With no goals scored, United seemed content with a draw. But with just five minutes to go, Fernando saw his chance and grabbed the ball.

In for the kill

He cruised his way down the field and skilfully fought off one opponent after the other. With a superb flick, he winged the ball home. "I never thought I'd do it", he said triumphantly.

Use a subheading to introduce a new idea.

Use powerful verbs – for 'ran', say 'galloped' or 'sprinted'.

Use quotes from competitors and spectators to back up your statements.

Dull... or exciting?

Here are two reports of the same event, but one is boring while the other grabs your attention. What makes the difference?

explanatory clauses

Record finish in freestyle finals

by V. Dull

The freestyle race began. The lead was taken by Emma, <u>who was in lane 1</u> and whose dive placed her in front. <u>She swam through the water</u> quickly.

Then, from lane 3, Verna came forwards. <u>She swam through the water,</u> moving her way forwards with <u>strong</u> arm strokes and feet movements.

boring adjectives

repetition

active voice

Record finish in freestyle finals

by V. Exciting

Splash! They <u>were</u> off! Emma in lane 1 got off to a great start. Her long dive put her into the lead. She glided effortlessly through the water, leaving behind a froth of <u>bubbles like a jet stream.</u>

Then Verna streaked forwards from lane 3. Soon she was inching her way forward with <u>swift</u> arm strokes and feet movements that barely <u>ruffled</u> the water's surface.

simile

adjectives

powerful verbs

RECOUNTING EVENTS IN DIFFERENT STYLES

Very often, what we write and how we write it depends on who we are writing for. For example, you would use different styles of writing to describe a visit to a theme park to your best friend or to your teacher.

Informal style

Your best friend Nadine loves going to the theme park. You'd write to her in a natural, chatty style – almost as if you were talking to her. You'd take for granted that she already knows lots of things about the theme park, so you wouldn't have to explain the rides to her.

FUN PARK
ADMIT ONE

FUN PARK
ADMIT ONE

REMEMBER TO USE:

chatty, informal style

25, Diamond Lane
St Albans
Herts
20 Nov 2006

Dear Nadine,
    I went to Adventure Towers yesterday with Mum, Dad and Susie. The coach ride took ages (as usual). The rides were fantastic as ever and there was a gigantic new roller-coaster that you're going to love. I thought it'd be scary but it was really awesome.
    For lunch we had pancakes, and that ice cream you adore. Yum! In the afternoon we went on a water ride. You should have seen Dad – he got soaked. Mum couldn't stop laughing.
    We had a really cool day. I'll ask Mum if we can go again when you're back from hols.
        Love Jane x x x

colloquial language ('scary' and 'awesome')

snippets of information about the writer

exclamation marks for emphasis

contractions ('you're' instead of 'you are')

76

Tip

Always use full sentences – even when you are writing in an informal style. It will make your work easier to read and keep the meaning clear.

Formal style

Your teacher asks you to write about your outing for a display of work aimed at parents. As you don't know the people you're writing for, the language you use should be more formal. You need to give more details since they may not know the theme park. To help the reader, you could include some subheadings.

Give facts rather than personal opinions.

My trip to Adventure Towers
Yesterday, my parents took my sister and me to Adventure Towers, <u>the largest theme park in this part of the country</u>. It is not always easy to find parking there, so we went by coach.

All sorts of rides
We tried out lots of different rides. Then we went on the new roller-coaster. It was huge and had lots of carriages with four seats across each row. It was frightening but also great fun.

Water everywhere
We had lunch in a restaurant overlooking the lake. After lunch, we went on a water ride that took us up and down slides and through tunnels. We were thoroughly wet by the end of the ride.

Time for home
We were too tired to do much more after the water ride. Luckily we <u>did not</u> have to wait too long for the coach back into town. We all enjoyed ourselves and had a very exciting day.

Use formal language.

ACTIVITY

Write recounts of a birthday party you've enjoyed for two people from this list:

- grandparent
- younger brother or sister
- pen friend from abroad
- school magazine editor

Springboard

Keep a diary. Each day, recount the day's events. Decide if you'll write in an informal or formal style. If your diary is 'for your eyes only' you may choose an informal style. However, if you want others to read it eventually, you could be more formal.

WRITING A CV

A CV gives factual information about your education, achievements and hobbies. It will help someone decide whether you are the most suitable person for a position, for example to take part in a scheme or be given an award, or, when you're older, to be offered a job.

Did you know?

The letters CV stand for the Latin words curriculum vitae, which mean 'the story of your life'.

Is a CV the same as an autobiography?

A CV gives the facts about what a person has done in their life. The facts are usually set out in reverse order with the most recent first.

An autobiography is the story of someone's life, written by that person. It includes observations and feelings, facts and opinions. It is written in the first person: 'I'. The facts are usually set out in chronological order.

Writing a CV

It's important that you keep your CV short and to the point. Don't forget that the person reading it will also be reading lots of other CVs. Here are some tips:

- Begin by writing your name, date of birth and contact details.
- List all the things you've done, both in and out of school. Start with your most recent achievement.
- Include as many things as you can that are relevant to what you are applying for. You need to persuade the person that you are the most appropriate candidate.
- List your favourite hobbies and pastimes.

Do include in your CV achievements, such as:
- I was awarded my gold swimming badge.
- My painting was selected for a competition.
- I helped organize a 'bring and buy' sale.

DON'T include these in your CV!
- My cat loves cheese.
- My pencil case is blue.
- I failed my maths test.

Research a celebrity of your choice (living or dead) and write their CV for them, listing their achievements and hobbies.

Springboard

Put the title 'Curriculum Vitae' at the top. Centring the type on the page looks good.

Curriculum Vitae

Name: Toby Mann
Date of birth: 4 April 1998
Address: Flat A, 66 Wood Avenue, Goodtown XX12 5RY
Telephone: 00101 5252

List your educational achievements from the most recent, ending with the earliest.

Education
April 2009: Passed with honours Piano Playing and Composition, Grade 1
January 2009: Won third prize in Goodtown' s Music Festival, 12 Years and Under category
December 2008: Played Jack in school production of *Jack The Giant Killer*
May 200: took part in interview about my school, published in the *Goodtown Gazette*

Hobbies:
Skateboarding, music and reading.

Include the names of two people who can recommend you, when you apply for a job.

References:
Mrs P. Shooter, Mr C. Saw

Tip

Type your CV on a computer. It looks neater and it can be easily updated and altered.

79

POWER OF PERSUASION

Writing that tries to persuade the reader to agree with what is being said is known as exaggerated writing. It is **biased** – it puts forward only one point of view. For example, a brochure advertising a holiday in a mountain chalet 'with magnificent views to the lake' avoids saying that you can only see the lake if you stand on a chair. An advert for an MP3 player claims that you can tune in to pop bands' live performances, but doesn't state that first you must buy an expensive card to slot into the player.

Twinkletoes
does the dancing for you!

Want to become a brilliant dancer in just TWO minutes? Then strap some Twinkletoes onto your shoes and get tapping.

You'll be a whirling, twirling disco star - and the envy of your friends.

Twinkletoes strap-on lights offer you the latest innovations in dance and rhythm technology.

Full money-back guarantee if you're not 100% thrilled with the results!

Order now while stocks last!

When to use exaggerated writing

People use exaggerated writing to try to convince the reader to, say, buy something that they are selling, such as a holiday, a new type of drink or a computer game.

Presenting exaggerated writing

Have a go at some exaggerated writing. Set out your writing in the form of an advertisement, a poster or a brochure, and make it as eye-catching as you can to grab the reader's attention.

• Use large and striking pictures.
• Vary the font size of your text.
• Write in the present tense to make it sound immediate and urgent.
• **Use positive language that makes the reader think their life will be improved.**

Word power

Choose your words carefully. Each word must make an impact. Rather than saying that something is 'good', use words such as 'brilliant', 'amazing', 'unique', 'wonderful', 'superb', 'fantastic' and 'one in a million'.

• Use lots of adjectives and superlatives – words such as 'idyllic', 'outstanding', 'coolest'.
• Present opinions as facts: 'Mrs Goochi says, "This is the best handbag ever!"'.
• Give your writing the stamp of approval of so-called experts with phrases such as 'leading experts agree', 'leader in the field recommends' and 'endorsed by'.
• Use technical or scientific words that sound authoritative, even though the reader won't understand them.

Use a software program to make a poster that looks really slick and professional. Set your text in different colours and fonts and vary the font size. You could advertise one of the following or invent your own product.

• A holiday destination
• A 'unique' hair product
• An environmentally-friendly car

Springboard

JUMPIN' BEENS

Live in concert
Your chance in a million to see the stars perform!

ONE NIGHT ONLY
8 May

The DISCO Centre is proud to present the sensational Jumpin' Beens performing hits from their latest album, Tweenie Beenies

'Tweenie Beenies, with its unique mix of up-beat backing tracks and amazing lyrics, is a winner...the best album to hit the music scene in years' Music Review

To book your ticket visit www.jumpin'beens.com or call The DISCO Centre on 145 39 09

Put the most important information at the top.

Provide a quote to back up your statement.

Give details of where to purchase tickets at the bottom of the poster.

INFORMATION WRITING

Imagine you've been asked to write a report on 'Animals of the Rainforest'. It's a topic that interests you but you don't know much about. Where do you start? Do you want your report to be about different types of mammals or all sorts of different animals including insects, reptiles and birds?

ACTIVITY

Have a mindmapping session with a group of friends. Write the words 'Rainforest animals' in the middle of a large sheet of paper. Then write on the names of the rainforest animals and what you know about each one. When your spidergram is finished, on another sheet of paper list the things that you need to research, such as: what other mammals live in the rainforest?, are there any rainforest insects?

Researching

Find out about your chosen animals, using information books and the Internet. If you're using books as reference, use the contents page and index to speed up your research.
Scan the text for key words:
'Poison-arrow frogs are brightly coloured. Their colouring is a warning to other animals that they are poisonous.'
Take notes. Write down only the words that are important e.g. frilly lizard = green, eats mosquitoes, hibernates.

frogs

toucans

rainforest animals

loudest land animal

monkeys

howler

spider

largest New World monkey

What we know
Monkeys, toucans, frogs live in rainforest

What we need to find out
What is a rainforest/where is it found? (for intro)
Insects
Reptiles
Other mammals

Starting to write

Organize your writing into sections so that, for example, all your information on toucans is under the same section.

• Use a subheading for each section.

• Write in the present tense since you are describing the way the animals are.

• Move from the general to the particular, for example 'Monkeys communicate with each other by making loud noises. Howler monkeys are the loudest monkeys of all.'

Useful words

Use words that relate to your chosen topic to make your writing sound accurate and factual. For example, for a project on rainforest animals the following words would be useful: canopy, camouflage, extinction, leaf litter, species.

Tip
You don't have to arrange the sections of your report in any particular order as they are not linked in a sequence.

Use technical words, such as 'habitat', 'herbivores' and 'primates'.

Start with general information.

Use adjectives to describe the animals, such as 'black' or 'dark red' hair.

Use subheadings to divide up the text.

Pick out an interesting piece of information and place it in a box outside the main text.

Write a caption underneath each illustration.

Illustrate your text with photos and labelled drawings.

Gorilla

The gorillas' habitat is forest areas of Africa. They are the largest of the primates, which are the group of animals that include monkeys, apes and humans.

Description

Gorillas have black or dark red hair. The adult male gorilla is called a silverback because his hair goes grey along his back.

Lifespan

Gorillas live up to 30 years.

Food

Gorillas are herbivores. They eat:

o   fruit
o   leaves
o   stems of plants

The gorilla is an intelligent animal.

PROJECT WRITING: ANCIENT GREECE

Suppose that a group of you has been asked to write a project on an aspect of Ancient Greece. Before choosing your topic, research all you can about Ancient Greece – from inventors, thinkers, writers and poets to architecture, the city-state and daily life.

Which area interests you the most?

Get ideas through a mindmapping session, and make a list of sections to include, such as farming, gods, festivals, medicine, myths. Organize your ideas into a spidergram, with a topic area, such as 'homes' or 'food' at the centre. Write down key words next to each section.

FOR SALE

Fine mud-brick and plaster period dwelling with tiled roof – in excellent condition.

- Spacious andron for entertaining friends
- Bathroom with new terracotta tub
- Large courtyard with well
- Mosaic floors throughout

Central Athens. Close to Agora, gymnasium and Temple of Apollo.
Early viewing highly recommended!
Offers over 5,000 drachmas

Which style?

When you've got enough information on each section, think about the different ways in which you could present it. For example:

- Newspaper report from *The Sparta Daily News* on the invention of the water clock
- Interview with Alexander the Great
- Advert for an Ancient Greek home
- Balanced report on whether girls should go to school
- Sports report on the Ancient Olympic Games
- A letter from a Greek child to their best friend

Daily life in Ancient Greece

The houses in Ancient Greek times usually consisted of two or three rooms built around a courtyard. A wealthy home might have two courtyards and an upstairs floor. The courtyard was the most important part of the home. That is where the family gathered to talk, entertain friends and listen to stories.

Children in Ancient Greece played with lots of different toys. Favourite toys were rattles, wooden hoops, toy animals and dolls made from clay, yo-yos and a horse on wheels that was pulled along. Children also enjoyed outdoor games such as juggling and playing on seesaws.

The Ancient Greeks loved to tell and listen to stories. They told many stories about their gods and goddesses and how the world was created. The most famous storytellers were the blind poet Homer and the slave Aesop, whose fables are still read today.

Ancient Greeks ate lots of vegetables and fresh fruit such as grapes and figs. They made bread from wheat and barley and kept goats for their milk, which they made cheese with. If they lived near the coast they ate fish and seafood. They did not eat meat.

Clothes were made from linen and wool. They consisted of a piece of cloth wrapped around the body and held together with pins and brooches. They wore sandals or went barefoot.

ACTIVITY

Turn this page of information into a report. How can you set it out so that it is easy to read, informative and eye catching?

Remember to :
- use subheadings
- put some text in boxes
- use bullet points and labels
- illustrate your writing with drawings or diagrams
- caption each illustration

SUMMING UP

There are lots of ways to write and present non-fiction texts. They include news reports, balanced reports, recounts and project writing.

Checklist

Here is a list of things to remember when writing non-fiction.

• Audience/purpose

Before you start, you should have some idea who you are writing for. Is your writing intended for a friend, a teacher or someone you don't know? The language you use will depend on who is going to read it.

• Presentation

The way you present your writing is important and will vary according to what you want to say. If it's a recount of a trip, you need to follow the sequence of events. If you're writing for your class newspaper, you need to start with the most important fact.

• Facts and opinions

Non-fiction is mainly about facts but it can also include opinions. Make sure that you distinguish between the two and don't present opinions as facts.

• Research

Make sure your facts are accurate. **Double-check** information you find on the Internet.

And don't forget to:

Take notes
- Have a mindmapping session to collect ideas.
- Use a spidergram, timeline or other device to structure your argument.

Organize your facts
- Start your writing with a heading.
- Use subheadings when you start a new topic.
- Use bullet points to list facts.

Illustrate your work
Include drawings, diagrams and charts to back up your information.

Get together with your friends to produce a school or class newspaper. It's a good idea to have one or two people in charge of each page. You could include pages on:

- school news
- other news
- sports
- book reviews
- puzzles
- interviews

Springboard 1

Springboard 2

Organize a reading club and ask each member to write a review of a book they've read. Keep the reviews in a folder or post them on your school's website, so that others can read them when they're wanting to choose a book to read.

Springboard 3

Write an information book with friends on a topic that you are all interested in. Working with a partner, each pair writes two pages on a particular aspect of the topic. For example, you might write a book on pop bands with pages on:

- when did pop start?

- survey of favourite pop bands

- balanced debate: is listening to music while doing homework helpful or harmful?

- mums', dads' and teachers' favourite bands

- in-depth look at one band

- the best-ever guitarist / drummer / singer

THE DRUMBEATS

Tips and techniques from a real writer

How To Write

LETTERS
AND EMAILS

Type your way to success !

Now YOU can write:

- fun and formal letters
- emails, postcards and invitations
- secret codes for penfriends

CONTENTS

ALL KINDS OF LETTERS

Ever since writing was invented, people have communicated through letters and other kinds of written messages. With the arrival of electronic mail (**email**), we still spend much of our time sending each other written messages. Here are some examples of ways we communicate in writing.

Informal letter

If you write to someone you know well, you can use a chatty **tone**, as if you can hear your voice talking to the other person. This is suitable for a catching-up, newsy letter to a friend or a thank-you letter to a relative.

Tip

Put 'regards', 'kind regards' or 'best wishes' instead of 'love from' if it's someone you don't know that well.

Dear Susy,
It was great to see you on Sunday...

...and they would love to meet up again soon.

With love from

Always start with 'dear' — or even 'darling' if it's someone you know very well!

*Use a **comma** after the person's name.*

Postcard

It's usual only to send postcards to good friends, family and neighbours, so they will be quite **informal**. There's a picture on one side and your message and the address of the **recipient** has to fit on the other. There's not much room, then! You will need to keep your handwriting small or not say much.

Having a fab time here in the mountains. Our hotel is just across a wooden bridge. It's really comfy but there's no TV. I don't really mind 'cos there's loads of things to do. Climbed up to the top of Craggy Hill today and paddled in a stream on the way down. Food's great. Weather's brill.
See you soon. Love, Carl.

*You can leave out the **greeting** to save space and jump straight in with the message.*

*Use **abbreviations** to save space.*

Formal letter

When you write to someone who you don't know that well, you don't want to write a chatty letter. You should use a more **formal** style.

Dear Mrs Dusty,
I really enjoyed my visit
to the Museum of...

Yours sincerely,

*The closing **phrase** is separated from your **signature** by a comma.*

Tip
In formal letters, start with
• Dear Sir (to a man)
• Dear Madam (to a woman)
• Dear Sir or Madam (if you don't know which, and can't find out)

Very formal letter

Sometimes you may need to write to someone whose name you don't know or choose not to use.

The name of the recipient and/or their job title comes first.

The Director
Stuffwells Taxidermists

Dear Sir,
I would like to find
out about the services
that you offer and...

Yours faithfully,

Put the name of the company above the greeting.

Tip
When you write 'Dear Sir' or 'Dear Madam' use the ending 'Yours faithfully'.

People tend to start emails with 'Hi', especially to friends and family.

Email

The fastest way to communicate in writing is by email. You send a letter typed on your computer keyboard to the computer of the recipient. They can then open your email and read your words on their screen. You can also send attachments (word files or pictures) tagged onto your email for the reader to open and look at.

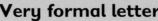

Subject: HOW R U?
From: Jade Jones < j.jones@urserver.com
To: Susie Smith < s.smith@supersupplier.co.uk
Hi Susie,
Just deleting old mails and reread yours. Sorry
I never replied – been soooo busy! How's things?
Have you heard from Jack? I saw him last
week at the rock festival. Took funny pic
(see attached jpeg).
See ya!
Jade

Shortened words and incomplete sentences are fine.

LAYING OUT LETTERS

Whether you are writing an informal letter or a formal one, there are different ways of laying out your letter, so that it is easy to read.

Tip

Put a sheet of ruled paper underneath your plain paper as a guide to keep your writing in straight lines. It looks better than writing on ruled paper.

Informal letter to a grandparent

22 Stables End,
ROCKINGTON
Shrubshire
TN80 4QT

The date goes on the left above your greeting.

Write your address in the top right-hand corner of the page.

17th January 2007

Dear Grandad,

Thank you so much for the money you sent me for my birthday. I'm going to spend it on...

Love from
Jon

*If you have paper with a **letterhead**, you only need to put the date before starting your letter.*

The Spinney
Long Lane
FAIRFORDHILL-ON-SEA

17th January 2007

Dear...

Springboard

Use one of the following addresses as inspiration for who you are, where you live and what you are writing about. Create a suitable name for yourself and for the person you are writing to. Make sure you lay out your letter in an appropriate **format**.

Highwire House
Juggler's Lane
Custardswell
Slopshire

Cutlass Cottage
Jolly Roger Road
Walkwell-on-Plank
Cornwall

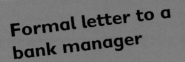

Formal letter to a bank manager

Write the recipient's address at the top left of the page.

The Manager
Fairford Bank
Whistle Street
FAIRFORDHILL-ON-SEA

Put your own address at the top right of the page.

The Spinney
Long Lane
FAIRFORDHILL-ON-SEA

13th April 2007

Don't forget the date!

Dear Madam,

*After 'Dear Sir/Madam', you may want to state the **subject** of your letter before starting to write it. In this case, it is usual to centre your subject. You could write in capital letters and underline it to make it stand out.*

<u>OPENING A YOUNG SAVER'S ACCOUNT</u>

I am interested in learning more about your YSA scheme as advertised in this week's *Fairford Gazette*. Please could you send me an application form at the above address.

Yours faithfully,

Molly Beer

Molly Beer

*SAE enclosed

When you address an envelope, start halfway down the envelope and left of centre. Begin each line of the address directly under the one above.

*SAE

SAE stands for 'stamped addressed envelope'. Including an envelope that is stamped and addressed to yourself encourages the recipient to reply to your letter at no cost to themselves. It is polite if you are asking someone for a reply or for them to send you something.

Molly Beer
The Spinney
Long Lane
FAIRFORDHILL-ON-SEA

Tip

Do not put an SAE into a chatty letter to a friend. If they intend to reply, they will happily pay their own postage as you are their friend. If you include an SAE to them they will probably be either offended, or feel pressured into writing – or both!

FINDING YOUR VOICE

When you write a letter, it is important to write clearly so that what you say will be understood. You don't have your voice or facial expressions to convey your message. As you write your letter, picture the person who will be reading it. Imagine how they will react to your words. From your opening line you set the tone of your letter. Make sure you continue to the end in the same 'voice' as you started.

Misunderstandings

When words are spoken face to face, the listener can see your eyes, and the expression on your face and judge your intention. If you say something that they misunderstand, you can correct your words straight away.

In a letter, the recipient can only judge what you are saying by the words you have written. They might misunderstand what you are saying. This is especially so in the case of jokes. Make sure you joke only to people who know you very well and understand your sense of humour. Otherwise they might not realize that you're joking and could be upset.

Tip

Re-read your letter before posting it, to make sure everything is clear. You could even **role-play** your reader's reaction when they open the letter, to help you to adopt their viewpoint.

If you are writing a formal letter to someone you don't know:

- Begin with 'Dear Sir' or 'Dear Mr Smith' (or 'Dear Madam' / 'Dear Mrs Smith').
- Use phrases, such as 'I would' and 'Please could you'.
- Don't use contractions, such as 'I'm' and 'won't'.
- Don't use slang words, such as 'fab'.
- End your letter with 'Yours faithfully' or 'Yours sincerely'.

If you write a chatty letter to a friend:

- Use their name or nickname, such as 'Dear Mo'.
- Use contractions, such as 'I've' and 'shouldn't'.
- Use lots of adjectives, such as 'cool' and 'fantastic'.
- End your letter with 'Love from...'.
- Don't forget to add some kisses!

Judging the tone

You have invited your friend to a party and she has said she can't come. You want to tell her you are sorry that she won't be there. Read these different ways of saying this in a letter. Which do you think is best?

I do think it's a shame you won't be at my party. I really wanted you there. You will miss all the fun.

I am disappointed you can't make my party. It won't be the same without you there.

What a shame you can't make it to my party. I understand why you can't come but I'll miss you. Let's get together next week and I can tell you all about it.

A. Sounds a bit moody and self-centred – the first two sentences both start with 'I'. She might think that you didn't understand that she really wanted to come to the party, but couldn't. This letter might make her feel guilty, which would be unfair as she was sad to miss the party.

B. Sounds a bit better than A. But the reader might think you are disappointed in her personally, rather than disappointed not to be seeing her at the party.

C. Sounds best of the three. It focuses on the reader rather than the writer. It suggests sympathy and understanding rather than blame. It also ends on a positive note, suggesting a fresh opportunity to meet.

Springboard

Pretend to be the party-thrower and try finishing off letter option C. (Begin the letter with 'Dear...'.)

THANK-YOU LETTERS

Thank-you letters can be very easy or really hard to write. A lot can depend on the following factors:

- What are you saying thank you for: a kind deed, a thoughtful present or a party you went to?
- How well do you know the generous person – very well, a little, or not at all?
- Did you expect the present or help, or was it a surprise?
- Did you like the present or party?
- Are you writing for yourself or on behalf of a group of people?

Being polite

What if Aunt Julie sent a present you hate – something too young or too small for you: an ugly doll with purple hair, a set of bath toys or a hideous sweater? How can you be polite about it?

Tip

Find something positive to say, however loosely linked to the present. For example:

- What a surprise those bath toys were! Mum will expect me to wash now – it's not natural!
- Thank you for that lovely top. My favourite colour! It must have taken you years to knit.
- Many thanks for the doll. I had fun choosing a name and decided in the end that Maxi will suit her best.

ACTIVITY

Try writing a thank-you letter on behalf of your class to a theatre group that recently visited your school. Things for you to think about include:

- What did they perform? What was special about their act?
- Did your class join in? If so, how?
- How did you and your friends react and respond?
- Would you like them to come again some time?

Begin:

Dear Actors,

I am writing on behalf of Class... following your visit to our school last week...

Springboard

Write a thank you letter for a strange present whose purpose you can't work out!

WORDS TO HELP YOU: fascinating, intriguing, interesting, unusual, fun

Thanking strangers

It might seem odd to write and say 'thank you' for a present to someone you don't know, but it can happen. Mums and dads have lots of friends. Perhaps one of them met you when you were a baby and still sends you a present each year. You don't know the person but you have to say 'thank you'. What can you write about?

Tell the reader the purpose of the letter.

Give reasons why she made an especially good choice. Phrasing the first reason as a question sounds friendly – as if you were talking to her.

13th April 2007

Dear Aunt Julie,

I am writing to thank you for the lovely scarf you sent for my birthday. Did you know yellow is my favourite colour? It's so warm and arrived in perfect time. I wore it when I went ice-skating with my friends last week.

Mum tells me you used to go ice-skating with her when you were my age. I wonder if you fell over as often as I did? Probably not – who could beat my record?

Next week we go back to school. I'll be in a new class with a new teacher. Everyone who was in her class last year calls her The Dragon. I hope my scarf has protective powers that save people from dragons!

Hope you are well and having fun.

With very best wishes,

Dale

PS Mum sends her love.

Shows you know who she is and suggests you are interested in her, not just her gift.

Offer something interesting for her to think about: a glimpse of what is happening in your life. The scarf gets another mention – not essential, but an added bonus!

Informal closing words are more friendly than 'yours sincerely'.

The letters 'PS' stand for postscript (Latin for 'after writing') – useful for adding afterthoughts, separating them from the letter's main purpose.

LETTER TO A PENFRIEND

A penfriend is usually someone you have never met. They live in another part of the country – maybe even the other side of the world. Or perhaps it is someone you met on holiday and you both decided to keep in touch. If English is not their first language, keep the language that you use when you write simple.

Tip

You don't want your letter to read like a page from a diary. Nor do you want it to read like an **autobiography** – 'My Life So Far'! Avoid beginning every sentence with 'I' (though it's fine to include a handful!).

Why write?

You are writing to each other to make friends. You could share information about:

- yourself, your home and family – any pets
- your school and home town
- your hobbies and interests
- what kinds of music and films you like

11 Bruton Street,
Wingford TT4 9BG

11th June 2007

Dear Carlos,

My name is Jake and I'm 11 years old. My sister, Molly, is two years older than me. She has a pet guinea pig and I have two rats, called Tricky and Nibbles. Sometimes we let them play together and they get on really well. Do you have any pets?

My best friend is called George. We both have games consoles so we can play together after school. ICT is my favourite subject at school. It's cool! I also like writing, which is why I wanted a penfriend. What's your best subject?

Tomorrow I'm going to the ten-screen cinema to see a new sci-fi film. I'll tell you all about it next time I write.

Hope to hear from you soon. Please tell me all about life in Spain!

Your new friend,

Jake

You want to learn the same sort of information about them, in the hope that you have things in common, shared interests, and will get on well.

ACTIVITY

Find out if your town is twinned with a town in another country. Write to a new penfriend from your twin town. Include information about your town and local environment in your letter. Ask a few questions about your penfriend, for him or her to answer.

Tips on finding a penfriend

• If your school has links with a school in another part of the country or abroad they may be able to help you find a friend to write to.

• If your home town is twinned with a town abroad, the Twinning Association may find you a penfriend.

• Write a letter to your favourite comic or magazine asking if another reader would like to **correspond** with you. (The magazine should not publish your address, but send on any **responses** to you.)

Signing off

You can't write 'Love from…' when you don't know somebody very well. 'Best wishes', 'All the best' or 'Regards' are all fine. You are opening doors to friendship without assuming you will be great pals too soon. When you first write to a new penfriend you will need to include your surname as you sign off. You don't need to include it in subsequent letters.

Springboard

Imagine that another planet has recently been twinned with Earth. Write a letter from an alien who lives on the twin planet. Write as if you were that alien, telling your human reader all about yourself and your planet. You might even enclose a recent 'school photo' of yourself!

LETTERS TO OFFICIALS

One reason that people write letters is to express an **opinion** in public, but why do people put their feelings into writing? And where do they send their letters?

TO TRY TO MAKE SOMETHING HAPPEN

Reasons for writing

You may want to write an official letter for one or more of these reasons:

TO HIGHLIGHT A PROBLEM, SUCH AS A SAFETY ISSUE

TO TRY TO PREVENT SOMETHING HAPPENING

TO COMPLAIN

Sending it off

When you write to express an opinion, you hope that someone will take notice and act upon what you have to say. This means it is important to send your letter to the correct person. It's no good complaining to the council about getting too much homework; they can't do anything about it! Don't write to your headteacher to complain about the cinema closing. It's nothing to do with her!

Tip

If you cannot find out whom to write to, perhaps the editor of the local paper will know. You could always write to the paper with your concern, in the hope that they might print your letter.

ACTIVITY

Imagine that your local council plans to close the play area in your local park and turn it into a golf course. With a group of friends, write a series of letters to the council and / or the editor of the local paper about the golf course proposal. Adopt the points of view of different members of the local community, such as:

• Local golfers. They think it's great – or most do. Some say they won't be able to afford the higher proposed membership fees.
• The local wildlife society. It is not happy. Its members say that rare insects and birds will suffer if the trees are cut down.

Remember that these will be formal letters, so begin 'Dear Sir/Madam' and finish 'Yours faithfully...'

PARK TO BECOME GOLF CLUB SHOCK!

Plans were unveiled today by Jobsworth District Council to turn Greendale Park and Leisure Amenity into a state-of-the-art 18-hole golf course. ~~residents were up in arms at the proposal of~~

Springboard

Write a letter to a celebrity asking them to visit your friend who has been in hospital for a long time. Explain why you chose them, how their visit will speed your friend's recovery and why they deserve a visit. This time, instead of 'Dear Sir/Madam', use the celebrity's name. End with 'Yours sincerely'.

Present the situation.

Express your opinion, explaining briefly why you hold your view.

Make a suggestion.

Request some specific action – including a reply to your letter.

23 Greendale View
Jobsworth

Jobsworth District Council
Jobsworth

16th June 2007

Dear Councillor Brown,

<u>TOWN PLANNING APPLICATION</u>

I am really worried about the plan to turn my local leisure park into a private golf club. I am a ten year-old who plays there regularly and I don't want this to happen.

My brother and I and all our friends have played there all our lives, as did my mum and dad when they were children. We also have swimming lessons and clubs at the swimming pool.

If the park and pool close we will have nowhere safe to play. The nearest swimming pool is ten miles away. For our safety, we must learn to swim because there are rivers and a reservoir nearby.

Golf players are mostly grown-ups who can drive out of town to play golf. Why don't you use wasteland where there would be plenty of room for an 18-hole golf course, and leave the rest of us to enjoy the park and swimming pool, and keep fit and safe?

Please take my suggestions seriously and talk about them at your next meeting. Please write and let me know what you're going to do.

Yours sincerely,

Make sure your whole letter fits on one side of a sheet of paper.

DRAFTING A REPLY

Sometimes you will receive a letter that needs a reply. It is often best to **draft** your letter first before you send it. Read this letter and think about how you might respond.

ACTIVITY

Draft a letter of response. Here are some things for you to think about as you draft your letter:

- Include a brief introduction: say who you are and where and how you came by the letter of invitation.

- Include a **paragraph** on your outdoor activity experiences so far.

- Try to answer all Mr Bold's questions.

- Think up good reasons to back up all your **statements**.

Dear Reader,

SPECIALIST ADVENTURE HOLIDAYS

Are you aged between 7 and 13?

Do you like challenging fun and adventure?

Have you ever wanted to learn new skills and test them to the limit?

Would you love to make new friends in an exciting environment?

If the answer to all these is YES, then you could enjoy a Specialist Adventure Holiday in a beautiful region of lakes and mountains with like-minded people of your own age.

We are offering ONE FREE PLACE on this holiday of a lifetime. If you would like to be considered, write and tell us what strengths you would bring to the experience and what you would hope to gain from the fortnight's fun. Also tell us which outdoor event you would most like to try and why: kayaking, caving, archery, white-water canoeing, mountaineering, sailing.

Write to Harry Bold at:

Specialist Adventure Holidays
PO Box 12
The Lake District

I look forward to hearing from you.

Yours sincerely,

Jane Gray

pp Harry Bold ←

The letters 'pp' stand for 'per persona' (Latin for 'for the person'). They are used when someone signs a letter on behalf of another person, in their absence.

- Write your own address and the recipient's in the correct places.
- Where will you put the date?
- Decide whether to write 'Dear Mr Bold', using his **title**, or 'Dear Harry'. What different effect will each choice have?
- Start a new paragraph for each part of your letter.

Draft a reply to one of these letters that you have received through the post:
- A request from your favourite pop star asking you to join their band.
- A letter from your best friend who has moved to Australia.
- A letter from an alien inviting you to visit planet Zog.

22 Dog Lane
Whippet-on-the-Wold
Lincolnshire

Specialist Adventure Holidays
PO Box 12
The Lake District

7th June

Dear Mr Bold,

I picked up a copy of your letter at a local leisure centre, and I am writing in the hope of winning a place on a Specialist Adventure Holiday this summer.

As an active ten year-old, I like lots of sports. Recently, I gained my bronze life-saving swimming certificate and would love to try scuba diving and canoeing.

I've always wanted to visit the Lake District, so I hope you will consider offering me a place. My teacher says I'd be good at kayaking but I can't afford classes. This holiday would provide me with the perfect opportunity to learn.

I do hope I have convinced you of my enthusiasm and look forward to hearing from you.

Yours sincerely,
Sam Smith

When you have written your draft, read it aloud.

- Are your sentences short and to the point? If you run out of breath reading a sentence, then it is too long. Break it up into two shorter sentences.

- Does your letter fit on one side of paper? If not, then find ways to shorten it. Cut out any waffle. Make sure you haven't said the same thing twice in different ways.

- Sum up what you have said in your final paragraph to remind Harry Bold of what has gone before.

SENDING POSTCARDS

People often send postcards to friends and relations when they go on holiday. But you don't have to be on holiday to send a postcard. You might send one to a friend to show them the town or area where you live. Postcards are also a useful way of keeping in touch or sending a short message.

Unique message

What you write on the back of a postcard makes it more interesting and personalizes it. As there is not much space on a postcard, it's often best to leave out a greeting. The name and address alongside make it clear to whom you are writing. Mostly, you can pitch straight in with your message: 'Wish you were here'? No, there must be something better than that!

Tip

When you send holiday postcards you can usually write more or less the same message on each one. However, if you are sending a postcard to two friends or relatives who will compare cards, remember to choose different pictures and think of new things to write on each card.

You could tell your friends about:
- a fascinating fact that you've learnt about the place where you are staying
- what you did yesterday
- what you hope to do tomorrow
- how you find the local people and their customs
- if you have had a chance to practise a foreign language
- what the food and accommodation are like and – if you must – what the weather's like!

As space is limited, you can miss out a few words, such as 'the' and 'I' – the reader is clever enough to work those out for themselves!

Paragraphs can be ignored, too.

Staying in a wicked hotel! It's got everything: pool tables, jacuzzi, sauna, pool – the lot! Tomorrow, going climbing on sheer rock-face – can't wait! They provide safety gear so I'll see you back at school next term, no worries!
Bye for now,
Charlie

Mr Simon Pomfrey
56a City Heights
BURNINGTON
BU8 5QT

ACTIVITY

Try designing your own postcards. Here are some ways you can make them:

- Draw and colour a picture on a rectangle of white card about 15 x 10cm. It can be a picture of anything; your pet, a place that you love or your house. Cover it with clear, adhesive film. On the other side of the card draw a line down the middle, a rectangle where the stamp goes and lines for the address, Add a title for the picture at the bottom.

- Design your postcards on a computer and print them out. You could use digital photographs of yourself or your friends and family, or photos of scenery. You could divide the postcard into quarters with a circle in centre, and put a different photograph – or Clip Art – in each section.

- Make a collage from things you have collected from your holiday: cut-outs from photos or brochures, tickets, menus, pressed leaves and flowers. Stick them onto a rectangle of card and cover with clear, adhesive film.

Tropical sunset, Bali

Springboard

Buy or make a postcard to send to someone who lives alone and may not get much post – for example, a grandparent who lives far away, a great aunt or uncle. You could even send it to a neighbour as a cheery surprise!

glue stick

SENDING EMAILS

Letters don't reach their destinations until at least the next day, which is why they are sometimes called 'snail mail'. By contrast, you can tap out an email in a few seconds, press a key, and click! – it's gone. Your recipient can read it almost immediately.

Replying to emails

To reply to an email that you have received, click 'Reply'. Your **correspondent**'s old message will appear, ready for you to type your reply above it. Now the Subject line of the email will say 'Re:' followed by the original header. 'Re' means 'about' – so your reply will be, for example, 'Re: Cinema Trip'. You can add your message, such as: 'OK. Meet you by popcorn stall.'

ACTIVITY

Try adding a signature line to an email. This could be your favourite catchphrase or quotation. In the 'Tools' drop-down menu go to 'Options', then choose 'Signatures' to create a signature. Click the signatures icon to add it to your emails.

Drafting

It is best to draft an important message in a computer notepad to cut and paste into an email later. Even if you write an email directly into your mailbox, you can save it as a draft, by going to 'File' then clicking on 'Save as Draft', rather than sending it right away.

Tip

You don't have to type a title into 'Subject' – but it helps the recipient to find your email again later and reminds them what it was about. It's useful if you exchange lots of emails with someone to be able to identify which is which when all the email titles are displayed in your inbox.

Formal emails

Some emails are formal – more like letters. The layout may be different but the language will be the same as a letter: 'Dear...', 'Yours sincerely...' and so on. The date and time you click 'Send' will appear automatically along with the Subject, so you don't need to type the date into the email message itself.

The email address of the sender.

The email address of the recipient.

Cc *stands for Carbon Copy: the email address(es) of other people who will receive copies of this email.*

Bcc *stands for Blind Carbon Copy: the email address(es) of people who will receive a secret copy of this email. (Only you and they will know they have a copy.)*

From:	dad@home.com
To:	jack@home.com
Cc:	jill@home.com
Bcc:	mum@home.com
Subject:	Re: surprise party

Subject is the title of your email – it describes the subject matter or content in a few words. Make sure your Subject reflects the content of your email – it should say what you are writing about.

Dear Mr Smith
Thank you for entertaining everyone at my party. The King Kong costume was really scary – Mum is making a good recovery!
Yours sincerely,
Jenna Jones
50 Willows Way, Langton WR2 3NJ

If you include your address, type it underneath your signature (typed at the end of your email) rather than at the top of your letter.

Emails to friends are generally casual. A typical greeting is 'HI!'

Tip

Springboard

Imagine two of your favourite characters from books or TV were emailing each other. Write an email 'conversation' – a series of emails exchanged between them.

PARTY INVITATIONS

An invitation to a special occasion is one of the nicest letters to receive in the post. Imagining a friend's smile when they open your invitation makes them among the most satisfying letters to write, too!

Informal invitation

An invitation doesn't have to be formal. It can be quite casual.

The Cedars
42 Long Drive
Bloxtown

16 August

Dear Phoebe,

I'm planning a fancy dress party with a cartoon characters theme and would love you come. Are you free on Saturday, 22nd September? The party starts at 5 o'clock at the Town Hall. Do let me know if you're able to come. Hope you're well and enjoying life. See you soon, hopefully.

Love,

Jenny

PS I'm thinking of coming as Snow White. If you're stuck for costume ideas give me a ring!

ACTIVITY

Try designing an invitation card on the computer.

- Design a letterhead using Clip Art or your own designs. Or cut and paste a photograph of yourself or your house to sit at the top alongside your address.
- Add a border that fits in with the theme of the party.
- You could print out cards with borders and write the **text** by hand to make your invites look more personal (especially if you have nice, clear, legible handwriting!)

Tip

If you are using a computer, you can easily print lots of copies of your invitation, changing the name of the person you're sending it to each time.

Tip

Formal invitations are often written in the third person –

'Miss Jennifer Smith requests the pleasure of your company'

rather than the first person –

'Dear Phoebe,
I'm planning...'

Springboard

Write the invitation that Cinderella never received from the Prince inviting her to the Ball. Design a splendid letterhead fit for a prince and write the invitation beneath it.

Miss Phoebe Phinn

Formal invitation

If you're planning a really posh party, this is the time to send out formal invitations printed on special cards.

*Miss Jennifer Smith
requests the pleasure of your company
at a fancy dress party
on Saturday, 22nd September
at The Town Hall*

RSVP
The Cedars
42 Long Drive
Bloxtown

5.00pm
Dress 'Cartoon Characters'

RSVP

These letters stand for Répondez s'il vous plaît (French for 'please reply'). The invitation may include a date by which the host or hostess would like to hear from you. For example:

RSVP 20th August

Replying

When you reply to a formal invitation it is correct to reply in the same style. If it is written in the third person, you should reply in the third person (although nowadays people often don't):

Phoebe Phinn thanks Jennifer Smith for her kind invitation and is pleased to accept.

20th August

Write the date on a line of its own at the end of your reply.

FANTASY LETTERS

You have learned a lot about writing letters. How about writing some in a fantasy situation? You can role-play, writing in the **persona** of a fantasy character or a character who, in real life, could not write the letter for themselves.

Here are some suggestions:

• Write a letter from one fantasy character to another

It could be a mermaid writing to Santa Claus, explaining about the absence of a chimney or Santa Claus writing to the mermaid to apologize for the socks he gave her last year (not much use if you have a tail!).

• Write the letter you wrote and never sent

Perhaps you wanted to have a moan to someone about something but in the end you decided it would hurt their feelings too much to send it to them. Or maybe you were writing to decline the invitation to be bridesmaid or page boy at your aunt's wedding, but decided you could cope with wearing a silly, frilly dress or shirt for a few hours, after all. Have fun writing the letter... but don't send it!

• Write a letter from a pet to its owner

Maybe the pet is complaining about its living conditions or its lifestyle. For example: you could pretend to be a hamster who complains that his wheel squeaks and he needs his cage cleaning more often; a guinea pig who complains about her diet (her carrots are soft and she would like some celery for a change); a dog who requests some new places to go 'walkies' with more lampposts and new smells – he's bored with the old ones.

• Write the letter you were never meant to see

You have found a letter which no-one intended you should ever read. Why? Perhaps it holds some dark secret about your ancestors – were they highwaymen? Or is it some other family secret? Or is it a pair of love-letters between your mother and father long before you were born, sounding all soppy and nothing like them!

ACTIVITY

When you have finished, try writing some letters of reply.

Springboard

If you enjoy writing stories as well as letters you could combine the two. Have a go at telling a story through an exchange of letters between two characters. Any other characters in the story will only be made known to the reader through what the two correspondents say about them.

Ask an adult to help you to melt candlewax to make a seal for the envelope.

Dearest Ma,

I be writing this note by candlelight as since I surprised that latest coach on the high road, not a mile from your cottage, I dare not show my face by day. It's not for nowt that they call your son The Second Dick Turpin!

Should anything happen to me afore we meet, your future is secure. The Third Oak holds some rewards three foot West of its trunk. Let it not be said that I let my dear Ma go hungry.

Do not expect me by day but if a masked man taps upon your window in the small hours, I beg you grant him access. It will be I, your own loving son,

Tom

You could try writing the letter in ink with a quill pen made from a feather.

To make the paper look old, add some tea stains. Ask an adult to brown your letter in a hot oven for a few minutes.

WRITING IN CODE

Ever since people learned to read and write, letters that needed to be kept secret have been written in code. Some codes are easier to crack than others. Here are some examples:

Codes that involve rearranging the layout of the lettering:

ACTIVITY

Try using one of these codes or make up a new one with a friend. To invent a letter code, write out the alphabet across or down a piece of paper. Then write your code letters or numbers beside each original letter. Now you can send each other messages to decode.

Earj ohni hopey oua rew elln. Extw eeki amh avingap artyw. Illy oub ea blet oc omed?

able to come?
week I am having a party. Will you be
Dear John, I hope you are well. Next

Dea rjo hni hop eyo uar ewe llN ext wee kia mha vin gap art yWi lly oub eab let oco me?

able to come?
week I am having a party. Will you be
Dear John, I hope you are well. Next

Here, in each sentence, the first letter of each word hops onto the end of the word before.

Raed nhoj I epoh uoy era llew. Txen keew I ma gnivah a ytrap. Lliw uoy eb elba ot emoc?

able to come?
week I am having a party. Will you be
Dear John, I hope you are well. Next

Here every word has three letters — but it is the same message as before. A capital letter shows when a new sentence starts.

Again, this is saying the same, but here each word is spelled backwards.

Codes that involve reading some words and not others – every third word, for example:

Bananas are dear today so Leah and I please will not meet up soon. Joe is not at home for the week. Oh well!

Dear Leah, Please meet Joe at the well.

Dear Leah, Please meet Joe at the well.

Tip

Single-letter words speed up cracking a code, so join 'I' and 'a' up to other words to make you code harder to crack.

Coded messages that can be read in the mirror:

Dear Leah, Please meet Joe at the well.

Dear Leah, Please meet Joe at the well.

A code that substitutes the next letter in the alphabet to represent each letter of the original message:

- EFBS MFBI QMFBTF NFFU KPF BU UIF XFMM

Dear Leah, Please meet Joe at the well.

Springboard

Create a **pseudonym** to conceal your identity. See if you can think one up that gives clues as to who you are really, such as an anagram of your name. For example, ALICE WARNER could sign herself RARE LAWN ICE.

HINT: To form an anagram, write the letters of your name on separate slips of paper. Jumble them up and see what new name you can create.

Or you could try combining your pet's name with a pop star, such as FIDO DIDO.

Tip

If you use numbers for your code, don't use them in order A=1, B=2, and so on. That's too easy to crack.

SUMMING UP

Here are some final points to think about when writing a letter.

1. Picture the person you are writing to as you write.

2. In an informal letter, write as you would speak – don't try to use sophisticated language just because it is written down.

3. Draft your letter first on scrap paper. Then you can concentrate fully on neat, legible handwriting for the **fair copy**.

4. Plan how to fold your letter so that it fits in the envelope. Practise with a spare piece first.

5. Always remember to date your letter – including the year.

6. Keep your sentences short and read them aloud to check they make sense.

7. Remember, if your letter begins 'Dear Sir' (or Madam), then it must end 'Yours faithfully'.

8. Keep letters to recipients other than your friends to one side of the paper.

9. Avoid starting every sentence with 'I...'.

10. Stop and think twice before pressing 'Send' on an email.

Here are some further suggestions for practising your letter-writing skills. Write a letter to:

- a child of the future – perhaps your great-great-grandchild who is not yet born

- the grandfather or grandmother who you never met

- a famous historical character, such as Abraham Lincoln or Florence Nightingale

- your favourite fictional character

- your future self. Seal and address the envelope and write at the top: NOT TO BE OPENED UNTIL YOUR 21ST BIRTHDAY

Imagine you have just moved house. You are missing your old home and friends. Write your first email to your best friend. You want to sound upbeat and positive, and tell them all about your new home and locality. At the same time, you want them to know you think about them a lot. Try to strike a happy balance as you draft your email.

Laura's room
Upstairs at No 5

June 5th
Dear Mrs Collins,
       Would you like to join me for tea this afternoon? Please RSVP by lunchtime.

Yours sincerely,

Laura

Imagine you are stranded on a desert island surrounded by sea. All you have is writing materials. A bottle floats ashore. You write a letter, seal it in the bottle and throw it out to sea in the hope that someone will find and read it. What will you say in your 'Dear Anybody...' letter?

Write a letter to a member of your family in a formal style, as if you didn't know them well. For example:

• A thank-you letter to Dad for cooking dinner (beginning Dear Mr...).
• A letter to your brother or sister requesting a tour of their room (beginning Dear Mr / Miss).
• An invitation to Mum to join you for tea.

GLOSSARY

Abbreviation Shortened word, such as Rd for road; Dr for doctor.

Active voice Shows that the subject of a sentence is doing the action.

Alliteration The repetition of the same letter or sound at the beginning of several words, within a phrase or sentence.

Anthology Collection of stories by different authors.

Article A piece of non-fiction writing about a topic in a newspaper or magazine.

Assonance Similar vowel sounds within words.

Author Person who creates and writes a book.

Autobiography A book written by someone about their own life.

Automatic writing Letting the words flow from your pen as you write, without stopping.

BCC Blind carbon copy – a secret copy of a letter sent to another person. Often used when sending emails.

Biased Showing favour to one side of an argument.

Bold Type that has thick, heavy lines.

Caption Writing that explains an illustration or photo.

CC Carbon copy – an identical copy of a letter or email sent to another person.

Character A fictional person in a book.

Chorus Words, or lines, repeated at the end of each verse of a poem or song. Also called a refrain.

Chronological Events set out in the order that they happened.

Colloquial Informal expressions and phrases used in conversation.

Column A piece of writing that is set to a narrow width. Newspapers are laid out in columns.

Comma A punctuation mark, used to show a pause.

Contraction Two words that are shortened, using an apostrophe in place of one or more letters.

Controversial A matter or event that people strongly disagree about.

Copyright The author's right of ownership of an original text.

Correspond To exchange letters or emails.

Correspondent A person with whom you exchange letters or emails.

CV A record that lists your education and achievements.

Dialogue Direct speech between characters.

Direct speech Writing words as spoken ("I love you," he said.).

Double-check To check a fact twice, using a second source of reference.

Draft A first try at writing something.

Drafting Rewriting a poem a number of times until it is properly finished.

Edit To alter or rewrite, often removing or replacing words.

Email Short for electronic mail.

Episodic Written in episodes (parts) which describe a series of events.

Explanatory Part of a sentence that gives extra clause information.

Fable A legendary story not based on fact, often with a moral or a message.

Facts Things that are true rather than imaginary or made up.

Fair copy Correct final copy of a letter that is ready to be sent.

Fantasy Imaginary creation which could never be real.

Fiction A story about made-up characters and situations.

Font The style of type used.

Formal Following conventional rules and using correct language.

Format Style, such as the layout of a letter on the page.

Free verse Poems that ignore the rules, and instead emphasize the expression of feelings or descriptions.

Genre A kind, or type, of writing, such as poetry or fiction.

Glossary A list explaining difficult or technical words, which is arranged in alphabetical order and placed near the end of the book.

Greeting The opening phrase of a letter (eg. 'Dear...').

Headline Title of a newspaper article.

Impersonal Written in the third person language.

Indented When words or a line of poetry are set further into the page from the left-hand side than the rest of the words.

Index An alphabetical list of subjects that can be found in the main text.

Informal Relaxed and casual, easy style.

Legend A traditional historical story sometimes believed to be fact but without factual evidence.

Letterhead Address printed at the top of a letter.

Metaphor A phrase which says one thing is another but isn't literally true, such as 'Sue's a mouse'. Sue isn't actually a mouse but might be shy or nervous like a mouse.

Mindmap To think of anything and everything related to one subject.

Narrative Another word for story.

Novel An extended story, usually divided into chapters.

Novella A short novel.

Onomatopoeia The use of words that sound like their meaning.

Opinion A personal point of view (rather than a fact).

Pace The speed at which the action happens.

Paragraph A division within longer text which contains several sentences on a similar theme or subject matter.

Passive voice Shows what is being done to the subject of a sentence.

Persona Character or identity.

Phrase A group of words within in a sentence.

Plot Plan of a sequence of connected events with an outcome developed from the start.

Positive Emphasizing what is good.

Pp Per persona – meaning 'on behalf of'. Used when a letter is signed on behalf of someone who is not there.

Protagonist Central character or hero to whom the reader can relate.

Proverb A saying with a moral to it that offers advice through sharing human experience.

PS Post script – meaning 'after writing'. Text following the main writing and after the signature. Useful for afterthoughts.

Pseudonym A false name or 'pen name' used by a writer.

Questionnaire A list of questions to be filled in by people, to gather information.

Quotes Writing the exact words that a person has spoken.

Recipient A person who receives (say, a letter).

Recount Retelling of events in the order that they happened.

Refrain Another word for 'chorus'.

Response A reply.

Review An account of a book, film, DVD, play or piece of music that gives the writer's opinion.

Rhyme This occurs when words have the same end sounds.

Rhyme scheme The writer's plan for using rhymes in a poem, for example rhyming couplets or ABCB.

Rhythm The beat, or 'music', in a poem.

Role-play Behaving as if you were another person.

RSVP Répondez s'il vous plait – meaning 'please reply'.

Scan Reading a piece of text quickly to find out the key ideas or words.

Sentence A series of words that make sense and include a verb (a doing- or action-word).

Sequence A list of things in a certain order.

Signature Someone's name, handwritten by themselves.

Simile A phrase that compares one thing to another using the words 'like' or 'as', such as 'Hard as nails'.

Spell-check A computer program that checks and corrects spelling.

Statement An account of facts, rather than opinions.

Storyboard To plan a story using a picture sequence of the main scenes.

Subclause A phrase within a sentence, separated by commas each side.

Subheading A title that has less importance than a heading.

Subject What you are writing about.

Summary A brief account giving the main points of a piece of information.

Survey Finding out opinions on a particular issue.

Syllable A group of letters that make a separate sound within a word.

Symbol Something that becomes a sign, representing an idea or meaning beyond itself.

Tense The form a verb takes to indicate past, present or future (such as was, is, will be).

Text Written words.

Thesaurus A gathering together – usually in a book – of words with similar meanings.

Title A person's status that appears before their name, such as Mr, Mrs, Miss, Ms, Sir, Lady, Doctor, Professor, Reverend.

Tone Your style of writing, which could be chatty (if you are writing to a friend) or more formal.

Verse A section of a poem separated by a line space on the page.

INDEX